ENGLISH ⊞ HERITAGE

Book of
Winchester

REFERENCE
ONLY

WITHDRAWN FROM
THE LIBRARY

UNIVERSITY OF
WINCHESTER

D0543188

This book is dedicated to those, past and present, who have studied Winchester – as residents, visitors, archaeologists, archivists and scholars. There is yet much to learn.

ENGLISH ⊞ HERITAGE

Book of
Winchester

Tom Beaumont James

B. T. Batsford / English Heritage
London

© T. Beaumont James 1997

First published 1997

All rights reserved. No part of this publication
may be reproduced in any form or by any means,
without permission from the Publisher

Typeset by Bernard Cavender Design & Greenwood Graphics Publishing
Printed and bound in Great Britain by
The Bath Press, Bath

Published by B.T. Batsford Ltd
583 Fulham Road, London SW6 5BY

A CIP catalogue record for this book is
available from the British Library

ISBN 0 7134 7446 7 (cased)
0 7134 7447 5 (limp)

KING ALFRED'S COLLEGE
WINCHESTER

REF

942.2735
JAM

02405954

(*Front*) West Gate before 1850. The area on the left had
been gardens from *c.* 1650 until the 1830s. The Plume
of Feathers (*right*) was demolished in 1938 (*photograph:*
John Crook; © Barbara Carpenter-Turner).

Contents

Illustrations

Colour plates

Acknowledgements

A study of 4000 years of Winchester's development inevitably requires a range of expertise beyond the ken of a single individual. Those with knowledge of Winchester's past have been unfailing in their support and unselfishness in providing materials and answering questions and I offer them my most heartfelt thanks. In particular Martin Biddle (Winchester Research Unit) and Ken Qualmann (Winchester City Archaeologist) have read drafts, and with the staff in their offices have supplied illustrations and saved me from errors. Barry Cunliffe and John Collis kindly commented on certain chapters. I would like to thank King Alfred's College for continuing to support local studies. My colleagues in history and archaeology have read critically and have generously answered questions from their own expert knowledge. My research students and undergraduates have lit new areas from their studies, and I thank them. Ann Bailey has calmly sought illustrations and done much besides. Barbara Bryant, Martin Henig, Edward Roberts and Elizabeth Proudman all offered expert insights. Illustrations are individually acknowledged, but I should particularly like to thank John Crook, Judith Dobie, Alejandra Gutierrez and Philip Marter for illustrative materials. At Batsford Charlotte Vickerstaff has worked wonders in ensuring that the often opaque world of archaeology is intelligible to the general reader. Peter Kemmis Betty (Batsford) and Stephen Johnson (English Heritage) have been warmly supportive. My family have been models of support and encouragement and I thank them unreservedly. In the knowledge that it is not possible to reconcile all areas of debate, I take responsibility for the text printed here.

Tom Beaumont James
Winchester January 1996

Preface

The study of Winchester is unique because progress has been made towards the integration of many sources at all periods, but especially in the complex Saxon and medieval periods in which archaeology, architecture, documentary and scientific analysis have all been pursued. The work of the Winchester Excavations Committee and its successor the Winchester Research Unit have been of key significance for over a quarter of a century, not only in archaeological recording, but also in laying the foundations for study of topography and documents.

This study introduces the major trends and results as presently known. From the author's point of view, documents, buildings, prints, drawings and photographs are as much artefacts as are pottery, environmental evidence and other products of earth archaeology. So far as possible in a text of this length, themes have been traced through: built environment, population and social structure, economy and religion. These are set in the context of archaeology.

1

Winchester: heritage reviewed

Why Winchester?

Winchester has a place in every history of England, most commonly as the 'ancient capital' associated with Saxon kings. After the siege of 1141 its fortunes were mixed. In the late 1980s, however, it was regarded as the richest city in Britain.

The city has been studied not only as a Roman settlement, as was usual in the post-war period, but since 1961 as an urban phenomenon through time (**1**). Archaeological excavation and historical surveys have illuminated the development of the city from the Saxon period onwards. This is particularly evident in a seminal series of monumental books unique in British archaeology: Winchester Studies. Combining archaeology, architecture, history and science, these studies comprise an unrivalled, integrated approach which has set Winchester apart from other cities.

It is only in the twentieth century that archaeology, as a professional endeavour, has added depth and new dimensions to antiquarian and historical studies. The monuments stay the same, but examination of their context through digging and post-excavation analysis has produced some extraordinary results: archaeology's contribution is discussed in the chapters that follow.

The first records

There is little documented reference to Roman Winchester. The first is by Ptolemy, writing in Alexandria *c.* AD 150, drawing on older information. Saxon accounts, especially the *Anglo-Saxon*

Chronicle, are helpful in providing a chronology – if not always an accurate one – for events such as the conversion to Christianity, the founding of the minsters and Viking attacks. Also, names of individual historical personages, such as Bishop Swithun (died 861x3; see pp. 46–7) and King Alfred (died 899), are mentioned (see Chronology pp. 121–3). Manuscript and pictorial evidence which can be specifically associated with Winchester, amounting to products of a first 'Winchester School', survives from the time of Alfred onwards. Administrative sources such as the Burghal Hidage (p. 41) provide insights into the defences and reorganization of the city in the ninth and early tenth centuries.

Although Domesday Book (1086) was kept at Winchester, no survey of the city of that date now exists. However, surveys of *c.* 1110 and 1148 exist, and these include significant retrospective material from which much about the city in the period immediately preceding the Conquest of 1066 can be deduced. These have been published by the Winchester Research Unit in Winchester Studies. The twelfth century witnessed the flowering of a second 'Winchester School' which produced the exquisite Winchester Bible, the greatest treasure of the cathedral library today.

National administrative records, notably those of the exchequer, begin *c.* 1150. Winchester appears incidentally in these and in the records of the writing office, the chancery. These official records, housed at the Public Record Office, London, contain much detailed material about

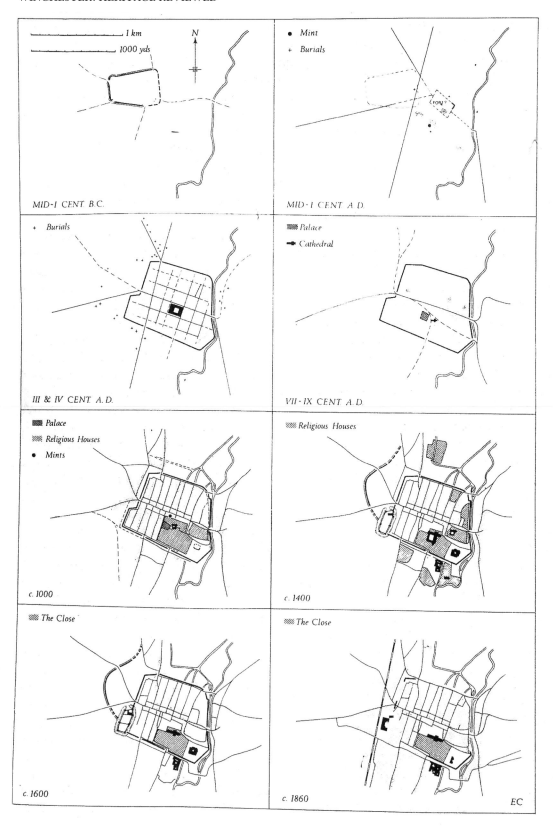

1 km
1000 yds
N

• Mint
+ Burials

MID-I CENT. B.C.

MID-I CENT. A.D.

+ Burials

▨ Palace
⊢ Cathedral

III & IV CENT. A.D.

VII-IX CENT. A.D.

▨ Palace
▨ Religious Houses
• Mints

▨ Religious Houses

c. 1000

c. 1400

▨ The Close

▨ The Close

c. 1600

c. 1860

EC

1 Eight phases of Winchester's development showing interpretations based on evidence collected to c. 1988. Modifications to our understanding since that date are noted on pp. 28 and 29 (copyright: Winchester Research Unit).

royal administrative preoccupations, such as visits to (and repair of) the castle and taxation accounts. The latter provide a basis for population figures, derived for example from the poll taxes of 1377–81. The fine series of city charters begins in the mid-twelfth century, concerned with the ancient privileges and town government (the gild merchant: see Glossary). A secondary series of charters from the fifteenth and sixteenth centuries deals with various forms of economic aid.

Charters form the basis of the city liberties and some are preserved among the city archives at the Hampshire Record Office (HRO). From the thirteenth century the city authorities began to generate records of its government, legal and financial affairs, including its land holdings. By 1417 Winchester city owned a large body of property, which increased substantially after the Reformation (see **colour plates 8** and **9**). Other institutions, including monasteries, the Hospital of St John, Winchester College and St Cross (a cartulary was rediscovered there in 1994), also held lands and their tenants were recorded.

Post-Conquest chronicles and annals report events in the city. They build on (and often build up) the Saxon and Norman history of the city, frequently making it hard, and sometimes impossible, to determine what happened when.

Travellers, gentlemen and antiquarians

Administrative records and chronicles were written for technical reasons, for example to apportion responsibility for taxation or rent. Many medieval chronicle writers, whose manuscripts are often found in the British Library, never travelled far from their religious houses. They presented evidence that they had heard, or read in earlier accounts, which they developed for their own purposes. Thus legends of King Arthur, Swithun and Alfred, scantily recorded by their contemporaries, developed later.

In the late fifteenth century and thereafter, the increasingly diverse administrative records continue to be very important, and include new sources such as probate inventories which detail the contents of individual properties room by room. They are joined by a group of materials, eyewitness accounts by visitors and antiquarians, which provide 'snapshots' of the city as it was at different periods, and furnish individual responses to the city previously only available through piecing together sources devised for other purposes. John Leland visited in 1540–1, just after the Dissolution of the monasteries. He found the city walled, with six gates, and refers to a dozen or so religious houses. Three of the suburbs were 'litle'; the eastern one – The Soke – was bigger, with two parish churches, both of which stand today.

The seventeenth century produced the first map of Winchester, by John Speed (**2**). John Trussell, a local historian of Winchester, witnessed the Civil War. A royalist, twice mayor and a comparative newcomer, Trussell (died *c.* 1648) was interested in the city's history and wrote *The Touchstone of Tradition*, a useful, if inaccurate, account of the early history of Winchester. The Restoration of 1660 revived interest in the city's past. William Schellinks, a Dutch topographical artist, visited in 1662. He admired recent additions to the cathedral, such as Inigo Jones's screen, now demolished, with its statues of James I and Charles I, which survive. His drawing of Winchester dominated by the ruined castle keep, shows the city as he described it 'within ... wide walls, which are now, like the castle, badly damaged. [The city] is large, but only thinly populated.' Henry Hyde, second Earl of Clarendon, was a courtier, who completed in 1683 *Some Account of the Tombs and Monuments in the Cathedral Church of Winchester,* to which was added a catalogue of cathedral charters compiled by the deputy record keeper at the Tower of London. Hyde's work and the catalogue were published in 1715.

Celia Fiennes, writing in the mid-1690s, clearly indicates the condition of the city, which had had its hopes of renewed royal status raised by

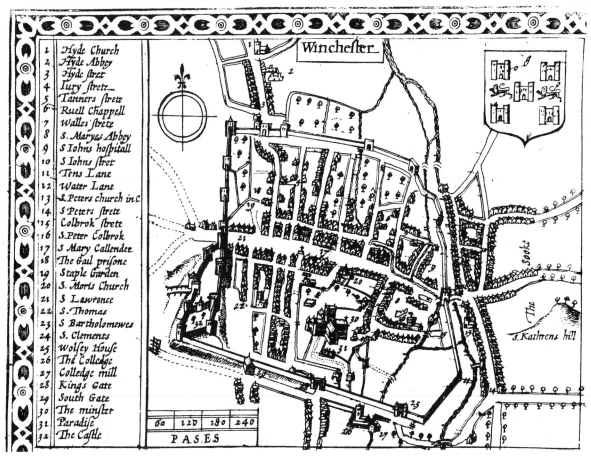

Map legend:

1. Hyde Church
2. Hyde Abbey
3. Hyde strect
4. Iury strete
5. Tanners strete
6. Ruell Chappell
7. Walles strete
8. S. Maryes Abbey
9. S Iohns hospitall
10. S Iohns stret
11. Tens Lane
12. Water Lane
13. S. Peters church in C
14. S Peters strete
15. Colbrok strete
16. S. Peter Colbrok
17. S Mary Callender
18. The Gail prisone
19. Staple Garden
20. S. Moris Church
21. S Lawrence
22. S. Thomas
23. S Bartholomewes
24. S. Clements
25. Wolsey House
26. The Colledge
27. Colledge mill
28. Kings Gate
29. South Gate
30. The minster
31. Paradise
32. The Castle

2 *Speed's plan of* c. *1611, enlarged from an inset in his map of Hampshire. North of the High Street, the Brooks area, comparatively bare of houses, contrasts with the flourishing eastern suburb (photograph: John Crook; copyright: Hampshire Record Office, 139M89, vol. 1, p. 3).*

Charles II but dashed by his death in 1685. She tells us much about the built environment: the streets 'pretty good, large and long, the buildings but low and old'. She admired the new houses in The Close and a model of the proposed royal palace, but was disappointed to see the palace itself unfinished. Fiennes, on the whole, deprecated historic or outmoded elements of the city. The cathedral and especially its monuments, Wolvesey (which her description suggests she did not visit), the ruined castle, the old-fashioned paths and potted plants of the Deanery garden, were criticized. But not everything old disappointed her: Winchester College chapel, cloister and library, the Renaissance replacement tomb chests of the Saxon kings and the choir-stalls in the cathedral she found appealing.

Eighteenth- and early nineteenth-century visitors and antiquarians

Daniel Defoe (*c.* 1725) was struck by the antiquity of Winchester, 'not only the great church ... but even the whole city has at a distance the face of venerable and looks ancient afar off'. He found the lack of decoration on the exterior of the cathedral disappointing and the structure 'plain and coarse', but he praised modern buildings: Winchester College 'School' (p. 98) and the new building at Wolvesey Palace, both built in the late seventeenth century. He was appalled at the ruination of the medieval bishop's palace at Wolvesey. He liked local society, both clergy and gentry.

A group of Cambridge gentlemen visiting in 1735 were, by contrast, impressed with the cathedral, dubbing it 'truly magnificent', and list the memorials to bishops with enthusiasm. They comment on the mixture of good and bad housing 'which contribute nothing to Beauty', though they were struck by the cleansing brooks which flowed openly through the streets. The following year saw the Buck brothers' panorama of Winchester (**3**) which records the city as the Cambridge gentlemen must have seen it.

The first measured map of Winchester was published in 1750 by William Godson (see **63** and **64**). The border shows certain important buildings and monuments, some of which Godson had surveyed for individuals and the corporation in an album produced at the same time (see **colour plate 10**).

William Cobbett visited *c.* 1830 and like his predecessors went to the cathedral 'that ancient and most magnificent pile' in particular to show his son, Richard, the tomb of William of Wykeham (died 1404). Richard observed, 'Why, papa, no one can build such places now, can they?' 'No, my dear,' replied Cobbett, 'that building was made when there were no poor rates; when every labouring man was clothed in good woollen cloth; when all had plenty of meat and bread and beer.' Such a conversation was characteristic of the enthusiasm for the Middle Ages, a feature of the incipient Gothic Revival, in which medieval architecture and life were favourably compared with that of the nineteenth century (**4**).

After viewing the cathedral the Cobbetts went outside the city to the north, where they were horrified to see in Hyde Meadow a county Bridewell (prison) occupying the site of Hyde Abbey, where Alfred 'that maker of the English name' had once been buried.

The Victorians

Such public interest as that displayed by Cobbett was mirrored by academic interest in the monuments of the past. This enjoyed a platform in 1845 with the meetings in the city of the British Archaeological Association in August and its rival, the more grand Archaeological Institute, in September. 'The room was crowded with fashionable company, among whom were many ladies,' trumpeted the *Illustrated London News*. A single national organization held a preliminary meeting

3 *The Buck brothers' panorama of 1736 shows Winchester College and the ruins of Wolvesey (left). Grand houses bracket the cathedral: (left to right) the Duke of York's House, St Swithun Street; houses in The Close and Wolvesey; Charles II's palace with Southgate Street below it and Pescod's Abbey House beside The Broadway. North of the High Street Penton's house dominates the residences which sprang up in St Peter Street and in the north-west area of the city. The eastern suburb flourishes. The Soke, Sir Thomas Fleming's early seventeenth-century house, old-fashioned with its timber frame (left), is beside St Peter Chesil church (John Crook).*

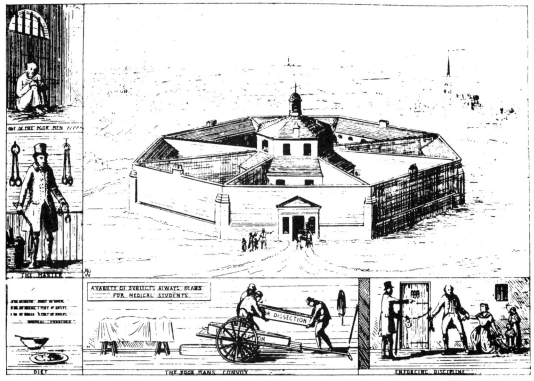

CONTRASTED RESIDENCES FOR THE POOR

4 Contrasted residences for the poor. Like Cobbett, Pugin unfavourably contrasted nineteenth-century experience with medieval. He does not label these drawings as Winchester, although a gaol in this style was to be built in the city (p. 108). Pugin was perhaps unaware that St Cross – which is clearly identifiable – was rebuilt in the fifteenth century, not for local poor, but for retainers of the aristocratic Cardinal Beaufort (p. 82) (A. W. Pugin: Contrasts, *2nd edition, 1846).*

at Canterbury in 1844 but had split in acrimony over the perennial question for archaeologists – publication; hence the two meetings at Winchester. The spirit of competition which characterized the Winchester meetings did, at least, stimulate interest in the city's history and antiquities. The speakers at the Archaeological Institute included Professor Willis, on the cathedral (5), Edward Hawkins on the ancient mint and exchange at Winchester, Sir Thomas Phillipps, J.G. Nichols and T.H. Turner.

The rapid publication of the proceedings, and the clear tide of public interest, was accompanied in 1846 by a proposal to found a museum. A meeting in October that year at the Corn Exchange resolved to found a museum for natural objects and also for materials illustrative of 'the customs, manners, and fashions of past ages'. The museum started life in Hyde School House as a county venture, but became the City Museum in 1851, in which year there were 2000 visitors. The curator from 1847 to 1871 was Henry Moody. It moved to the vacant house of the governor of the county gaol in Jewry Street, and thence to the new guildhall in 1874. A second museum, which still operates, was opened in the West Gate in 1898.

The Ordnance Survey produced a large-scale map of the city in 1872, on which many of these buildings can be identified. The gentry who had encouraged the museum were again active in the establishment of the Hampshire Field Club and Archaeological Society in 1885, which still regularly publishes primarily archaeological, architectural and historical material.

The coming of the professionals

The twentieth century saw the tradition of observing the city and noting chance finds translated into a policy of organized, intrusive excavation. Twentieth-century figures have not merely read about or observed ancient sites in the city, they have dug them up on an unprecedented scale. Some of this work has been research, such as Martin Biddle's excavations near the cathedral, at Wolvesey and elsewhere in the 1960s, some rescue, such as the City Archaeologist's work at Woolworth's or International Stores in the High Street, or The Brooks excavations of 1987–8 (see 7). An early stage in this change of emphasis was the establishment in 1903 of a new City Museum in The Square, created by Alderman Jacob's Museums Committee. This was one of the very first purpose-built museums in the country.

Between the wars archaeology was overseen by Sydney Ward-Evans (died 1943), the city's 'honorary archaeologist'. Ward-Evans was an amateur who had been encouraged by Edith Wilde, then honorary curator of the City Museum and herself an authority on the city's historic weights and measures. Observation by Ward-Evans of demolition sites and holes in the fabric of the city was invaluable for future archaeologists. Working unpaid and on his own he began to map out the city's archaeological past, depending for sustenance on donations of food from the *Hampshire Chronicle,* for whom he wrote. On the Iron Age site at St Catharine's Hill, J.N.L. Myres, the former Winchester College schoolboy and subsequently lecturer at Christ Church, Oxford, undertook excavations with C.F.C. Hawkes, which were published in 1930, and revised by Hawkes in 1976.

Meanwhile at the museum honorary curators were succeeded in 1947 by a professional. The first holder of that post was Frank Cottrill, who served for over twenty-five years until his retirement in 1973. He organized the collections and instigated an increasingly systematic archaeological study of the city and district. Cottrill, and his wife Eleanor, who was the county archivist,

5a *The British Archaeological Institute met in the finely decorated St John's Rooms in The Broadway in September 1845. The Lely portrait of Charles II, now in the Guildhall, is above the dais; the speaker seen here with the wand was probably Professor Willis (Author's collection).*

5b *The same room in 1983 (copyright: RCHME).*

6 *Martin Biddle on the Wessex Hotel (cathedral car-park) site in 1961 preparing a plan of a burial from the New Minster cemetery (copyright: Winchester Research Unit).*

brought about a transformation in the study of Winchester's past. Frank Cottrill was well connected in archaeology. He had worked with Mortimer Wheeler before the war and had taken over Gerald Dunning's position examining the archaeology revealed by building development in London, and, like Dunning, was a drawer of pots. He knew Kathleen Kenyon from Leicester, where he worked before coming to Winchester.

Sprung from the tradition of inter-war archaeologists, Cottrill saw that a new generation had to be encouraged. Three of these young men have since become professors of archaeology. In the 1950s John Collis was still a schoolboy when Cottrill encouraged him to excavate; Barry Cunliffe was another young and talented Hampshire archaeologist who came to excavate in Winchester before 1960. Martin Biddle was a Cambridge undergraduate, excavating a Roman villa at Twyford, when he met the curator and was invited by the city authorities to excavate the site of the Wessex Hotel in 1961 (6). Biddle, encouraged by Roger Quirk's remarkable prediction of the sites of the Saxon Minsters, then formed the Winchester Excavation Committee and excavated for a further ten seasons until 1971. In Cottrill's time work at Winchester came to command major national and international attention.

Since 1972, the post of city archaeologist has been filled by Kenneth Qualmann, who has continued to excavate, largely in a rescue capacity, as rapid development has engulfed the city. Since 1990 rescue has stopped as government-funded excavation has given way to commercial backing under the recommended guideline known as PPG 16. Archaeology is now planning-led.

Digging, driven by excavation seasons, limited funds and developers' necessity to begin building, is over comparatively quickly. The products of the excavations (plans, sections, photographs etc. as well as the finds themselves) require many years of expert analysis, and often demand at least as much funding as the original excavation to prepare and publish the results. The records and finds are all to be found in the care of the City Museum, where Elizabeth Lewis, an authority on timber-framed buildings, was curator from 1973 to 1996.

Major excavations

The locations of the major excavations in the twentieth century are shown in **7**. This select summary is designed to help the reader through the maze of local terminology, by relating sites mentioned in the text to periods and excavators.

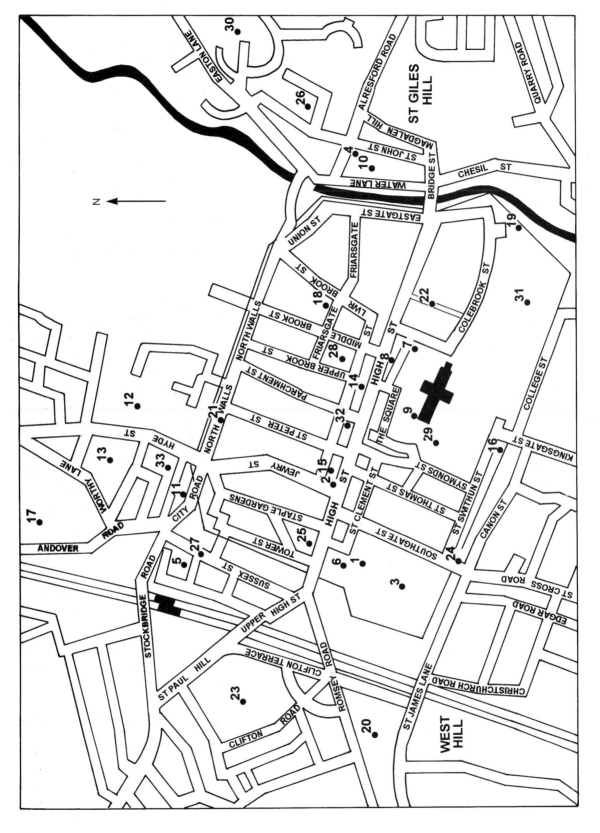

7 *Map of Winchester identifying archaeological sites and streets (drawn by Philip Marter).*

KEY
1 Assize courts
2 Barclay's Bank (George Hotel)
3 Barracks
4 Blue Boar
5 Carfax
6 Castle Yard
7 Cathedral car-park
8 St Maurice Church
9 Cathedral Green
10 Chester Road
11 City Road
12 Hyde Abbey
13 Hyde Street
14 International Stores
15 Kingdon's workshop & back of Royal Oak
16 Kingsgate Street
17 Lankhills
18 Lower Brook Street
19 Magdalen Almshouses
20 Mews Lane
21 North Walls
22 Nunnaminster (St Mary's Abbey) & Abbey Passage
23 Oram's Arbour
24 Southgate Street
25 Staple Gardens
26 St Martin's Close
27 Sussex Street
28 The Brooks
29 The Close
30 Winnall
31 Wolvesey Palace
32 Woolworth's
33 Victoria Road

Prehistoric sites
St Catharine's Hill (Hawkes and Myres before 1930)
Oram's Arbour (Erdberi) and Staple Gardens (Biddle 1964–7; Qualmann 1990s)
Carfax (Qualmann *c.* 1985)
Twyford Down (Qualmann and Wessex Archaeology 1993–4)
Berewick Field (Qualmann 1993–4)

Roman sites
St George Street (pre-1955; Cunliffe 1955–7)
Cathedral Green – the forum (Biddle 1961–70)
Lankhills cemetery (Clarke 1967–72)
Wolvesey (Biddle 1963–71, 1974)
International Stores, High Street (Qualmann 1986)
Brooks (Biddle 1963–71; Qualmann 1987–8)

Saxon sites
Winnall (Meaney and Hawkes 1960s)
the minster sites on the Cathedral Green and at the Wessex Hotel (Biddle 1961–70)
St George Street (Cunliffe 1950s)
Nunnaminster (Qualmann *c.* 1980)
Staple Gardens (Qualmann 1990s)

Medieval sites (c. 1050–1550)
housing and churches at The Brooks (Biddle 1962–71 (**8**); Qualmann 1987–8)
St George Street (Cunliffe 1960)
Wolvesey Palace (Biddle 1963–71, 1974)
the Castle (Biddle 1962–3, 1967–71; Qualmann 1980s, 1990s)

The contribution of archaeology

Archaeology has deepened understanding of the city's past. For the prehistoric and Roman periods we depend on archaeology for evidence. There is nothing to see on the surface of the Iron Age site at Oram's Arbour, and yet excavation and non-intrusive methods, such as resistivity survey, have provided a mass of information (p. 27ff). At St Catharine's Hill earthworks are upstanding (see **11**), but only by excavation could they be elucidated. Increasingly sophisticated techniques of typology and science have furnished date-ranges for evidence from the earth. Structures such as the Saxon minsters have been rediscovered after centuries underground.

Knowledge of the city's past has been sharpened by excavations which have uncovered some 5 per cent of the city's archaeology, according to present knowledge of both the historic area and the depth of deposits. Winchester excavations may not equal the area which has been exposed for example in York, but work in Winchester began comparatively early.

The range of materials discovered at Winchester and the depth of the analysis which sets archaeology in a proper perspective of history, architecture and other disciplines, are major achievements of British scholarship. In the pages that follow, the extent is highlighted to which archaeology with associated disciplines has

8 *Work in progress in 1964: Lower Brook Street, looking south-west. This area revealed domestic accommodation of post-Conquest date (house XIII shown here). Biddle pioneered open excavation: the baulks are still in place at this stage, with tags identifying the stratigraphy (copyright: Winchester Research Unit, 3021A).*

broadened perceptions of the city's past. In this study there is a place for royal Winchester, for its major monuments and exotic finds. Equally there is a place for more overtly archaeological topics: suburbs, houses and the built environment, industry, commerce, diet, funerary practice and burial.

2

Prehistory and Venta Belgarum

to *c.* 450

Landscape and location

This chapter looks at the prehistoric landscape of the Itchen valley and the engineered landscape occupied by Venta Belgarum. It was the Romans who made Winchester unequivocally urban. Archaeology has provided proofs of that urban identity: a concentration of population, a complex economic and social structure, organized religion and an influence over the area beyond its walls.

Winchester is at a narrow point on the flood plain of the River Itchen, with chalk hills rising both to the east (St Giles) and the west (West Hill) (**9**, **10**). Prehistoric populations occupied the higher ground, perhaps attracted to the area by a fordable place in the river, yet deterred from valley-bottom sites by marshy land of the kind still to be seen when walking south of the city through the Meads towards St Cross. The valley bottom was composed of a series of islands amid meandering streams that constituted the Itchen, which may have been navigable in light craft from the sea to this point.

Pre-Iron Age

So far as is known, the vicinity of Winchester was not a focus of population in the early Neolithic period. There is a marked increase in activity in the form of flint and stone tools and Beaker pottery from the Later Neolithic and Earlier Bronze Age both within the walled area and on the surrounding hills, for example a Beaker vessel found in 1892 at Mews Lane west of the city. Significant increase in settlement evidence to the east at Winnall, to the south at Twyford Down, and on the West Hill, is suggestive of foci of activity including agriculture, domestic occupation and burials, beginning around 2000 BC and continuing into the Later Bronze Age (see Chronology, p. 121).

The Iron Age

Evidence for the Early Iron Age (700–300 BC), from the area of the later walled city and its immediate vicinity, is predominantly agricultural: field systems, plough soils, a grain-drying hearth. People settled sparsely on the chalk downs, for example to the west of the present city, in the Middle Iron Age, *c.* 300–100 BC. The slopes of the Itchen valley continued to be used for agriculture. Two major foci of Iron Age settlement developed, at St Catharine's Hill to the south of the present city and at Oram's Arbour, which was referred to in medieval documents as 'Erdberi', to the west. St Catharine's Hill is a hill-fort: Erdberi an enclosure at the junction of a north–south route west of the Itchen, with an east–west hill trackway (**colour plate 1** and see **10**).

9 (*p. 24:*) *Location maps of Winchester (drawn by Alejandra Gutierrez).*

10 (*p. 25:*) *Contour plan of Winchester showing east–west cut (drawn by Alejandra Gutierrez).*

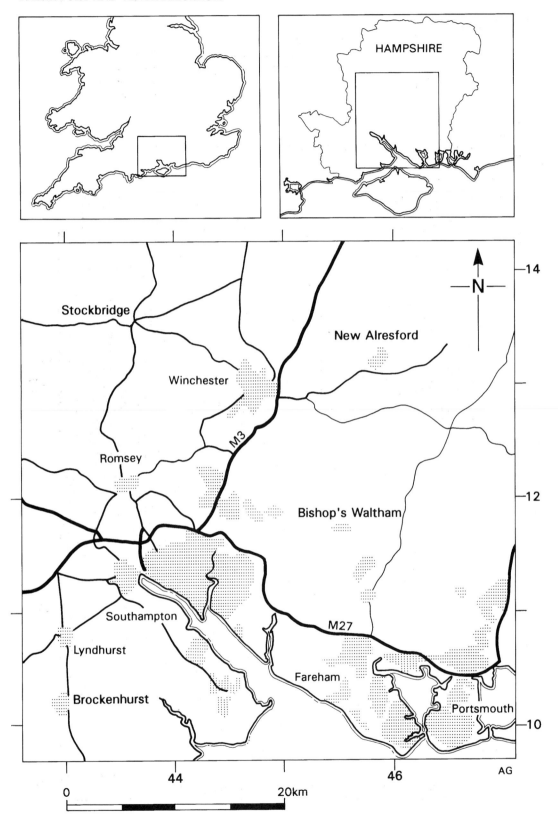

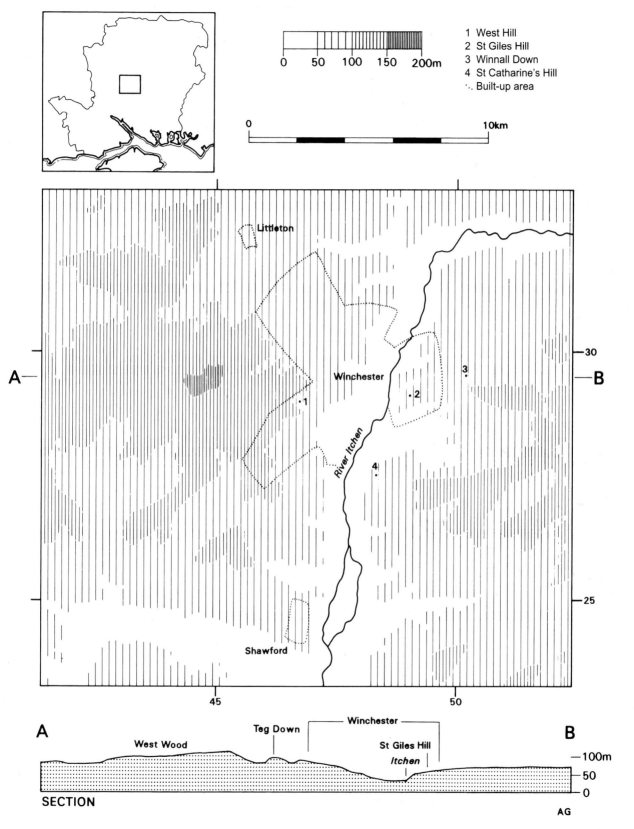

11 *St Catharine's Hill from the air in 1969. The Iron Age earthworks are clearly visible, together with their landscape of ancient fields. Compare this with* **colour plates 1** *and* **12** *(copyright: Winchester Research Unit).*

St Catharine's Hill

St Catharine's Hill was and is encircled by Iron Age earthworks (**11**). Iron Age pottery and arte-facts excavated there were published in 1930 (p. 21). It was demonstrated through dated pottery types that the entrance to the hill-fort was destroyed by fire and the site abandoned at the end of the Middle Iron Age, perhaps about 100 BC. The hill-fort dominated the eastern side of the valley of the Itchen. By the time that the pottery sequence ends on the hill, a corresponding pottery series had been established on the west side of the valley at Erdberi. It has been suggested that, as elsewhere, the higher eastern community, at St Catharine's Hill, was defensive, the lower western community, at least in the Early Iron Age (700–300 BC), unenclosed. Was St Catharine's Hill ever residential, or was it a refuge in time of crisis? It was probably a centre of economic exchange comparable with the hill-fort at Danebury, the best-known analogous site in Hampshire. However, as excavation concentrated on the defences, the nature of occupation inside the earthworks of St Catharine's Hill remains unclear.

Erdberi (Oram's Arbour)

There were settlers across the river from St Catharine's Hill in and around Oram's Arbour from the Early Iron Age to the beginning of the Middle Iron Age (600–300 BC). Excavations at Carfax, north-west of the city, for example, revealed rectangular 2 by 3m (6 by 10ft) structures built with upright wooden poles and associated with gullies, possibly field boundaries, suggestive of a mixed economy.

Excavation has revealed that this area, north-west of the city, was enclosed between c. 300 BC and 100 BC. Ditches and their upcast banks, no longer obvious to view, have been sectioned and dated by pottery. The Middle Iron Age settlement (300–100 BC) at Oram's Arbour is significant in both the length (1.7km/1.06 miles) and the scale of the rampart and ditch (c. 7.25m/24ft wide and perhaps 4.25m/14ft deep) of the defending earthworks. This enclosure was 20ha (50 acres) in area, which made it a prime defensive earthwork in southern Britain, equivalent in area, if not in strength of defences, to a site such as Maiden Castle (Dorset).

The Arbour enclosure may have brought together disparate farmsteaders who had settled in that area, possibly to create a more easily accessible refuge than that across the river at St Catharine's Hill. However, the creation of such a substantial earthwork is strongly suggestive of some driving force behind it, for example of a tribal leader. Such an interpretation accords not only with ancient writers, but also with recent arguments about Iron Age social structure put forward by Barry Cunliffe, who knows Winchester archaeology well.

Towards the eastern end of the Oram's Arbour enclosure, a comparatively dense occupation pattern of Middle to Late Iron Age date (300 BC–AD 43) was discerned on the Staple Gardens site, where roundhouses and other structures, in sequence of occupation, were excavated. In the Late Iron Age (after 100 BC) there was some industrial activity which was later buried beneath the western part of the Roman settlement (12), but a higher concentration of activity has been found to the south, outside the enclosure.

Iron Age coinage, such as an Atrebatic piece (early first century AD: see Glossary) found in the north-west quarter of the city, may have circulated in Winchester as money, although there is the possibility that such objects were expensive gifts perhaps distributed by tribal leaders. Extended economic links and complex trading activity are indicated by Ptolemaic and Gaulish coins (the latter paralleled at Hayling Island temple to the southeast), remains of sea-fish, querns from Lodsworth (West Sussex) and regional pottery types.

Links with the Continent in the Late Iron Age led to the arrival in the area of the Belgae from northern France or Belgium, who were to give Venta Belgarum (now believed to mean 'market place of the Belgae') its name. Whether they came as economic migrants, invaders, or as refugees from Caesar's invasions of the first century BC, is still debated – especially as Belgic pottery, which would give substance to the place-name evidence, has not been found at Winchester. That the Romans chose Venta Belgarum as their name for Winchester suggests that they believed the Belgae had occupied this area. Perhaps, more significantly, if this was the market place of the Belgae, then the site of that market was probably Oram's Arbour.

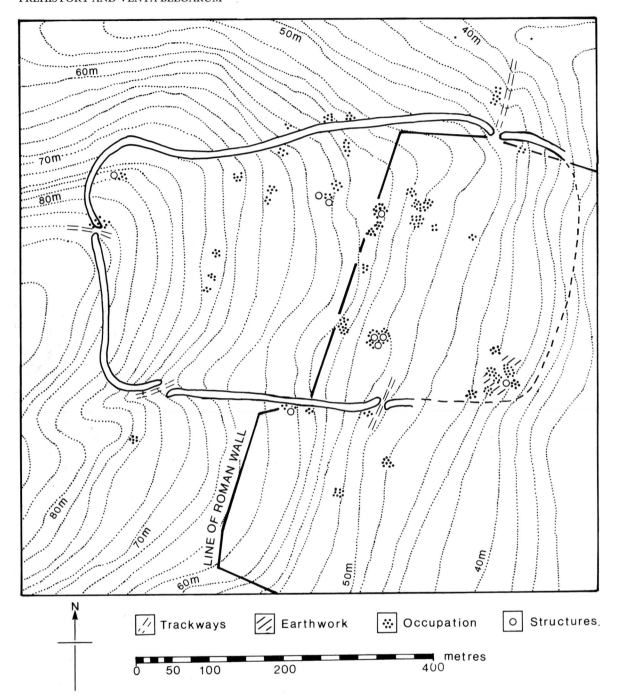

N

Trackways   Earthwork   Occupation   Structures.

metres

0   50   100   200   400

12 *Oram's Arbour (Erdberi) Iron Age enclosure. Recent excavations have revealed additional entrances at the north-east and south-west with associated trackways (cf. **1**) and broader occupation patterns (after Qualmann 1993, redrawn by Judith Dobie; copyright: English Heritage).*

13 *The River Itchen originally flowed further westwards than today (cf. **1**), around one or more islands. The southern boundary of the Iron Age enclosure at Oram's Arbour may have abutted the western bank of the river, in the area east of the present St Peter Street (after Qualmann 1993, redrawn by Philip Marter).*

The precise extent of the Oram's Arbour enclosure, and its functions, are still being explored, in particular its eastern boundary now buried beneath the area of the later walled city. East of St Peter Street (**13** and see **7**) the natural geology below archaeological layers has never been seen and a steep slope there may prove to be the eastern limit of the Iron Age enclosure.

Oram's Arbour is difficult to categorize precisely: it is not a hill-fort, nor does it meet all the criteria to be an *oppidum* or major enclosure. Although dominating a river crossing, it was

perhaps enclosed substantially earlier than the first century BC, the usual date assigned to the foundation of British *oppida*.

The end of the Iron Age

While some evidence survives of industrial occupation on part of the Arbour site in the period immediately before the Roman invasion of AD 43, the enclosure experienced a reduction in permanent settlement in the Late Iron Age. No evidence has yet been found that it was a centre for trade or religion at that period. Its impact on

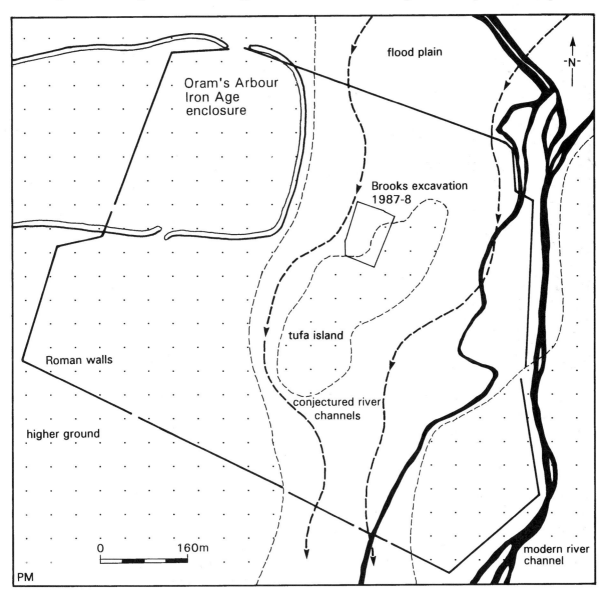

the planning of the early Roman settlement resulted from the existence of the Arbour's large earthworks.

Recent work at Berwick Fields to the north-west of the city has identified Late Iron Age roundhouses, trackways and grain storage pits, with continuity into the Roman period. Pits and field systems were also found at Twyford Down. Maybe with the abandonment of St Catharine's Hill and the scaling down of the Arbour, there was a slackening of centralized control in the Late Iron Age which on the one hand led to the scattering of population, and on the other made society more vulnerable to Roman invasion.

The Romans arrive

Following the invasion of AD 43, Winchester became one of the first Roman settlements: the evidence suggests a date of *c.* AD 50 for Roman occupation on the west bank of the Itchen and on a tufa (see Glossary) island in midstream. Characteristic straight roads were built by the Romans north towards Silchester and north-west towards Cirencester; in time six Roman roads radiated from Venta Belgarum. The layout of these roads particularly to the north of the city (see **1**) may hold clues for the transition from Iron Age to Roman settlement. Perhaps within decades of the invasion, and at the latest by AD 200, the Romans diverted the Itchen and bridged it to the east of their settlement, ensuring the future of Winchester as a centre of communication by road north–south and east–west across the river at the then lowest bridging-point. The Roman bridge and its attendant gate at Winchester, to the east of the city, were sited further south than the present city bridge (see **13** and **78**).

Excavations have shown that there was a sequence of Roman settlements at Winchester, but conclusive evidence of an early Roman fort has not been found. Early Roman Winchester inter-locked with, and in part overlaid, its Iron Age predecessor in the north-western area of the city. The two settlements used the same north entrance (see **12** and **13**), but whether the Romans made any use of the Iron Age defences is unknown.

Defences

The first Roman ditch and rampart defences ran along the northern, western and southern sides of the city; the location of the eastern defences, if there were any, at this early date is uncertain. The western bank and ditch included a 60 by 245m (200 by 800ft) salient where the defences jutted out south of the western entrance to the city at the highest point (see **13**). The reason why there was such a considerable deviation in the otherwise largely regular defences is a mystery. The salient is Roman in date, for excavations at the Castle Yard in the 1960s established this beyond doubt. Also within the salient, remains of a building with a tessellated floor were observed in 1683 by Sir Christopher Wren. The salient respected a structure yet to be identified, but it is uncertain whether this was a house, evidenced by tesserae, for a Roman administrator before the *civitas* (see p. 31) was established after *c.* AD 70, or a military area (although little military evidence has been found), or possibly even a theatre.

The extent of the first Roman defences is also uncertain, but a number of phases has been revealed by excavations, notably at South Gate, which suggest a foundation date of AD 75 (**14**). One of the anomalies of Winchester's street plan within the walls is that the north and south gates lay so far west on the city defences (see **13**). This suggests that the early Roman defences were focused further west than their later Roman and medieval successors. It seems likely that the early earthwork defences were part of a broadly sym-metrical settlement towards the west of the area eventually walled in. About AD 60, timber build-ings on at least one site between the High Street and St George Street were consumed by fire and early deposits sealed by a burnt layer. Excavation suggests that eastern banks of the Iron Age enclo-sure may have been levelled; or that the burnt structures marked the eastern limit of the early Roman settlement.

The defences of *c.* AD 75 were amplified and extended by a second series of earthwork defences *c.* AD 180–200 which included protec-tion along the river on the east and which

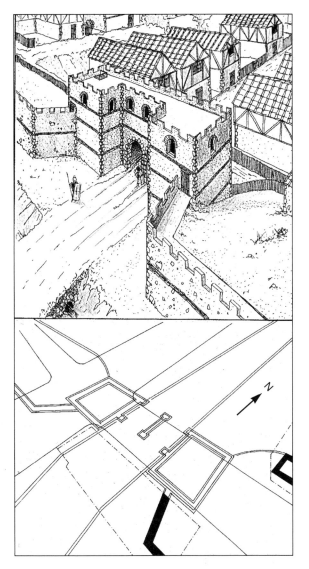

14 *Reconstruction and archaeological plan of the South Gate. The plan shows the excavated return wall and latrine. Little is known of the gate itself apart from observations in pipe-trenches. Note the medieval/modern site of Southgate Street, further west than their Roman predecessors. The central passage and gate lie under St Swithun Street (after Winchester City Museums; redrawn by Philip Marter).*

displayed. Fourth-century bastions were discovered at South Gate (1971). Garden walls between St Swithun Street and Canon Street follow the line of the southern Roman walls, and continue on the north side of College Street; north of the city at North Walls similar boundaries follow the line of the walls (see **7**).

Civitas status

The break-up by the Romans of the extensive kingdom of Cogidubnus, a client king of theirs, may have been the catalyst for the development of Venta Belgarum as the urban focus of a *civitas*, or Roman administrative regional centre, and as a thriving town. When he died late in the first century AD, Cogidubnus was probably the owner of the palatial villa at Fishbourne outside Chichester (West Sussex), where the main phase of building is dated to just after AD 70.

His kingdom may have been inhabited by three different peoples: in the north based on Silchester (Atrebates); in the east based on Chichester (Regnenses), and in the west based on Venta Belgarum (Belgae). On his death a reorganization of the region occurred: the western element became a *civitas* based on Venta Belgarum and is thought to have stretched westwards towards Bath. This might help to explain the arrival in Winchester of Bath stone found in Roman contexts (p. 43).

Major building works in and around the city followed *civitas* status. An administrative centre was created, based on a forum, which contained shops, offices and a basilica. The orientation of this major building is not known for certain but its site lay north-west of the current cathedral, either north-south across the western end of The Close, or to the south facing the High Street – although a north-facing basilica would have been rather dark. Buildings stretched northwards into The Square, where massive foundations have been picked up adjacent to the site of the City Museum. Evidence was recovered in the 1960s from the north and south ranges of the offices and shops which bordered the forum: to the south on the Cathedral Green site and to the east

completed the circuit. A stone wall was cut into them in the third century and medieval walls engulfed Roman ones in numerous campaigns of rebuilding. The line of the Roman walls is found in property boundaries today, to the east at The Weirs, where a scrap of Roman walling is

ANTONINVS AVG

15 *Fragment ?'NTO' of an inscription, perhaps from an imperial dedication to one of the Antonine emperors (see Glossary), in which it is set here. It is the largest lettering known from Roman Britain. Found in Middle Brook Street in 1957, its scale – 29cm (11½ in) – might link it to the nearby basilica (after Winchester City Museums, redrawn by Alejandra Gutierrez).*

at the Wessex Hotel site. Fragments of masonry have been recovered in excavation, for example part of an inscription, which suggest that these buildings may have been very substantial (**15**). Overall, such evidence as that from the administrative hub of Roman Venta, taken with the evidence of the defences (above, pp. 30–1) indicates increased significance betokened by major building programmes which developed in and after the final quarter of the first century AD.

For Winchester new status may have triggered civil engineering works. The aim of these works was to enable an extension of the city eastwards, perhaps as an open city on that side, on the valley floor of the Itchen. Much archaeological evidence supports this. Excavations, in the Brooks in the 1960s and in 1987–8 as well as under Woolworth's in the High Street, have shown that the Romans transformed that area of the valley on which Winchester now stands with drainage channels, and levelled the area by extending the islands.

To bring this extended platform into being the Itchen was redirected (as the Romans also did to rivers at Chichester and Cirencester) further to the east to enable the chalk island(s) to be consolidated. Alluvial deposits found both east and west of the Brooks are not so abundant further east, as was discovered at the Magdalen Almshouses site. Excavations have revealed substantial drainage channels in the Brooks.

The Roman street grid
The axis of the Roman street grid came to be east–west, although evidence from The Brooks

excavations may indicate an early north–south road along the island which later had the forum at its south end. The reordering of the city in the late first century possibly involved the extension of the street grid eastwards from the western and central area already established.

The clean yellow/orange surfaces of these streets, swept on behalf of the Roman administration until after AD 350, when rough cobbling and patching is found on various sites in the city, not only makes them easily recognizable in the archaeological record, but is a substantial indication of the rise and fall of Roman administration.

Cemeteries and population
Cemeteries can provide a basis for discussion of population number and ethnicity. It is the exotic which marks out graves, and thus it is often possible to say more about apparent immigrants than locals.

From cemeteries, so lacking for the Iron Age, and from other evidence such as distribution of houses, it is possible to speak with some authority about the population of Roman Winchester. By analogy with estimates for other Roman towns of known area, the inhabitants of Venta may have numbered 3–4000 in the second century AD. This is fewer than the number estimated for the walled area of Winchester in the medieval centuries, but substantial for a Roman town in Britain. Two reasons support this scale of population. First, the Romans did not apparently fill the 550,000sq m of the city, especially in the western area. Second, the Romans created a garden city. Evidence of wide corridors, courtyards and gardens is plain to see on Roman sites throughout the city, certainly in the mid-Roman period, but whether they packed the city more densely in the first and fourth centuries has not been demonstrated.

Roman law demanded that burial should be outside city walls. Extensive cemeteries have been found north, south, east and west of Winchester. From the cemetery north-west of North Gate, at Hyde Street and Victoria Road, finds included cremations and burials dating from as early as AD 50 up to *c.* AD 175, some with coins suggestive of soldiers' cash wages. Could these include Romans who conquered Britain in AD 43? The Romans subdued a native population, and the discovery of a horse burial in the bank and a pig's head in this extra-mural cemetery hint at native burials and Celtic feasting: natives were obliged to follow Roman burial laws.

The northern graveyard extended for 500m (1640ft): its size suggests that Roman Winchester was populous. At Lankhills, towards its northern extremity, 451 burials were excavated, almost all dating to *c.* 310–410. From the eastern cemetery 110 well-stratified graves were excavated at Chester Road, and a further 40 at St Martin's Close, largely of fourth-century date (**16**). These included an elaborate high-status burial monument over an interment with a lead-lined coffin; such a monument is an unusual find in Winchester.

An element of the southern cemetery has been excavated west of South Gate. To the south-east there were graves at Milland Road, while at Grange Road, rich first-century graves contained bronze and glass vessels, a shale platter and pottery, perhaps relating to a villa rather than to the city (**17**). Elements of a further cemetery or cemeteries have been discovered west of the city. Cemetery evidence suggests some growth in population in the fourth century.

Cemetery evidence, for example at Lankhills, has been adduced to suggest the presence in Winchester of foreigners from beyond the

17 *A costly copper-alloy jug, ht. 15.2cm (6in), perhaps imported from Campania, from a grave at Grange Road (south of the city), dated AD 85–95. The grave may have been associated with a rural settlement rather than with the city itself, and is among indications of a flourishing villa culture – Roman, or romanized Belgic – in the hinterland of Venta Belgarum soon after the Conquest (copyright: Winchester Research Unit).*

bounds of the empire after *c.* 350, precisely the period when the city's phase of Romano-British occupation characterized by conspicuous consumption was ending. Graves of foreign men and women, both mature and young, were identified by grave-goods, which included ornaments, brooches and beads as well as evidence of male or female activity – warriors' knives and belt-buckles or spindle-whorls.

Grave-goods associated with incomers have been used to show integration, for their adornments were increasingly British (better quality

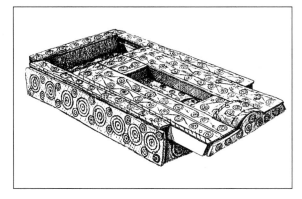

16 *Bone comb-box from a fourth-century grave at St Martin's Close (eastern cemetery). The comb in the box was of antler (drawn by Judith Dobie, English Heritage).*

than those from their native region), and their individual grave practices came to resemble those of the natives. The origins of some of these people who were buried at Lankhills have been proposed as the eastern Danube region in Hungary, beyond the imperial frontier, perhaps the area occupied by the Sarmatians. Such foreigners are likely to have come to the city as officials and soldiers, perhaps in a protective role connected with a *gynaecaeum*, or imperial workshop, which perhaps produced clothes for Roman troops in Britain and Germany. A *gynaecaeum* is known from a documentary source at 'Venta', perhaps Venta Belgarum.

Between 390 and 410 a further group of foreigners, identified from their grave-goods as 'Saxons', appears. This is arguably the earliest group of Saxon graves identified in England, showing artefactual associations not only with north Germany, but also with the Upper Thames valley, around Dorchester, which with Winchester was to play a significant role in the subsequent development of early Wessex. As is so often the case in archaeology, voices have been persuasively raised against the immigrant theory. A group with Saxon affiliations may have been connected with a late fourth-century official or military structure found in the south-east of the city at Wolvesey – and paralleled at Dorchester-on-Thames.

Society and housing

From the mid-first to the mid-fourth century there is plenty of evidence for spacious Roman town houses with roofs covered with stone or tile, stone and rubble walls, and mosaic floors, underlaid by hypocaust heating systems (**colour plate 2**). These houses had painted walls and glazed windows, features shared with rural villas, which sprang up in the countryside after AD 43, and which have been excavated, for example at Sparsholt and Twyford.

In Winchester there were timber dwellings, perhaps with wings, around a central garden or courtyard; double-corridor-type houses constructed of timber over a masonry base – occupied in the third century; a porticoed house of early fourth-century date with mosaic floors, hypocausts and a stone-tiled roof, and an impressive courtyard house, perhaps with a colonnaded courtyard and mosaic floors, of the fourth century (**18**). Such houses were found at The Brooks, although no one house had all the features listed above and there were variations in quality. The great floral mosaic pavement found

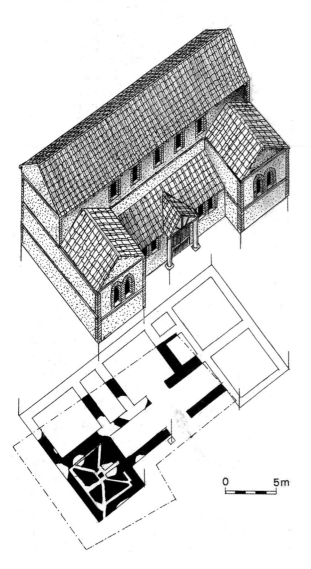

18 *Archaeological plan and reconstruction of a spacious Roman house (insula XXIII.3: see Glossary) of c. AD 300. The comfortable, porticoed house contained a hypocaust, with its stokehole (left) (after Winchester Archaeology Office; redrawn by Philip Marter).*

in insula XXIII house 1 appears to have been of late second-century date and is of the highest quality. It was not the first mosaic in Winchester, for black and white mosaics are known from the late first century and later at Wolvesey, Lower Brook Street and elsewhere. The pavements in house XXIII.3 on The Brooks were considerably later in date than at XXIII.1 and are less artistically accomplished. Altogether fragments of a dozen pavements and more are known from Roman Winchester.

There is increasing evidence of a varied population from the early Roman period onwards. Agricultural activity has been identified on The Brooks island from the first century, with slight timber structures interspersed between layers of cultivation material. Large private residences on both sides of a street in The Brooks were certainly in existence after AD 150 and may have been built earlier. The Romano-British elite developed an interest in urban living in second-century Venta Belgarum, as at Verulamium and Silchester, and their town houses remained in use throughout the third century.

The fourth century saw these second- and third-century dwellings replaced at The Brooks by a house whose dimensions have been compared favourably with the most opulent houses in Silchester. However, the later fourth century saw the decay, demolition and adaptation of Winchester's great town houses. Mosaics were roughly patched, a hearth created in a corridor, and layers of slag and charcoal confirm industrial activity. Some house sites were abandoned altogether, reduced to stub walls projecting above a layer of dark earth which began to accumulate around AD 400. Clearly there was a steep decline in the economic and social status of those who lived in this area of Venta, and it seems likely that this may have been true of the city as a whole.

Religion

An indication of early Roman religion at Winchester was a small 'Romano-Celtic temple' of contemporary date with the nearby forum, *c.* AD 100. Both were found on the tufa island in the

19 *The Romano-Celtic goddess Epona, or a worshipper, displaying a characteristic* mappa *(napkin) and key. Statuette in common oak (from Britain or Gaul), ht. 18cm (7in), c. AD 150–275; found in a well at Lower Brook Street 18m (59ft) south of a Romano-Celtic temple of soon after AD 100 (copyright: Winchester Research Unit).*

Itchen, the temple at Lower Brook Street. A wooden figure of a goddess, possibly Epona, or a worshipper, was recovered from this area of excavation (**19**). An altar was found in 1854 in Jewry Street, inscribed to Italian, German, Gallic and British mother-goddesses (*matres*), and is likely to be of early second-century date. Antonius Lucretianus, seconded for duty by the provincial governor, is mentioned on it as sponsor. He is unlikely to have been a native, and the altar was doubtless associated with soldiers.

Excavations of graves of a significant number of people at the Lankhills cemetery provided an opportunity for an examination of religious practices associated with the dead. Graves were largely from the fourth century, which was a time of transition from paganism to Christianity in

Britain: both Christian and pagan graves were excavated.

Up to *c.* AD 350 comparatively little account was taken of the ultimate destination and ease of passage of those who died, although provisions for the journey and some vessels were provided. As the century progressed more valuable offerings were placed in graves, which indicate observance of rituals and emphasize belief in an afterlife. Ornate combs appear among the artefacts, while the provision of money was perhaps to pay the ferryman to take the dead across the Styx. However, this evidence from Lankhills was not matched by finds at the Victoria Road part of the same cemetery – although probably later than Lankhills – where there were virtually no gravegoods, a situation mirrored at Chester Road in the eastern cemetery. Such discoveries hint at different status or beliefs among those buried in the city's cemeteries. However, dating is not precise and may be a factor in the distinctive evidence.

Because of the early fourth-century date of many of the graves at Lankhills, the overwhelming alignment of the graves with the head to the west could as likely be the result of the influence of the sun cult (*Sol Invictus*) on late Roman religion as of Christianity. Among the few gems found in Winchester is a glass one showing a bust of Sol. However, grave-goods such as a platter with a possible chi-rho motif on it could be evidence for Christianity *c.* AD 330–50. In this case the Christian artefact seems to be associated with a group of graves, perhaps those of a family group, distinct from the general burials at Lankhills. These are early dates for Christian evidence, for Constantine, the first Christian emperor, died in AD 337. From very much the same period, the earlier fourth century, a chi-rho monogram was found on a tile built into the corner of the hypocaust in house XXIII.3 at The Brooks (see **18**). However, less than 2m separated this tile from two jars containing animal bone, fish bone, eggshell and mussel shells, apparently placed in the new hypocaust as a pagan offering.

Paganism was a powerful force in Roman Britain, and may have become still more firmly entrenched *c.* AD 350–400 as political circumstances became more uncertain. From *c.* 400 a striking piece of evidence of paganism was found at the 'cenotaph' at Lankhills where evidence of a stout wooden coffin with a male skeleton, remains of a large dog with its legs in the air, a second dog, dismembered, and five bronze coins, not to mention the burial of a decapitated young man with a coin in his mouth, were excavated from the same grave. Cremations at the same date were undoubtedly pagan. Decapitations, of which there were several from the period after *c.* 350, might have been punishment for criminals, but those of a two-year-old child and of old women – not otherwise found in the cemetery – carried out *post mortem,* could have been connected with liberation of the soul.

Finally, burials petered out in the early fifth century, following a descent into disorder from orderly alignment of the Lankhills graves, while the latest graves at Victoria Road were shallow and more haphazard in position than previously.

Pottery and other artefacts

From the period of the invasion, until the late fourth century, there is continuity of occupation in Winchester, evidenced and dated by a full coin-sequence, and supported by a sequence of diverse pottery types. Occupation evidence begins in the reign of Claudius (died AD 54) with a mixture of imported samian ware from Gaul, and other imported pottery including jars and jugs, mixed with some comparatively coarse native wares, which included jars.

What appears, from the quantity and distribution of the vessels found together, to have been the contents of a samian ware shop of the mid-second century, was excavated at the International Stores site on the High Street. The first-century mixture of imported wares such as the samian, found in the rich Flavian graves south of the city, and very localized pottery, gives way to a more diverse type-series by the third and fourth centuries. New Forest and Oxford pottery is found in the city together with a widely distributed coarse-tempered ware of unknown origin. Fragments of glassware also appear, including bases of stemmed glasses suggestive of wine drinking. Trade networks encouraged exchange and brought wealth.

Decline

Perhaps before AD 300, and certainly after c. 350, grand buildings were being demolished and fragments such as a section from a mighty stone column and a moulded stone bracket from the façade of a substantial building were found in a well filled in around AD 300 together with other high-status objects such as a pewter jug. All the known Roman town houses, numbering more than a dozen, go out of use at this period.

An increase in burials in the Winchester cemeteries after AD 350 was accompanied by a shift in the nature of the settlement away from large stone buildings towards more flimsy wooden ones. The focus of occupation may have changed from within to without the walls at that time.

Some elements of the economy of the city possibly continued to flourish, or may have been developed, helping to sustain late Roman Winchester, for example the textile workshop (p. 34), which may have existed c. 350, supplied with wool from sheep on the downland around the city. The bulk of evidence, however, points to problems in the city by the middle of the fourth century.

In addition, the full coin-sequence in parts of the city breaks down: whereas certain sites north and west of the High Street produced fewer coins, elsewhere the sequence of late fourth- and fifth-century coinage continues. This suggests that some sites ceased to be occupied around AD 370, although this may have been a result of changing foci of activity.

The end of Roman Winchester

Flickerings of urban existence in Winchester continued perhaps until AD 400. Archaeology shows clearly that the city of the second and third centuries underwent comprehensive change. On many sites the period following the Roman occupation is sealed by a black clayey soil usually 15cm (6in) thick but sometimes up to 0.7m (2ft), containing sherds of broken Roman pottery, and indicating that vegetation covered the remains of Roman buildings for a very considerable period. It is doubtful that this 'dark earth' constitutes agricultural layers, for many Roman structures demonstrably protruded through it, although horticulture remains a possibility. Recent research has suggested that it may be possible to identify layers in this dark earth, and that its existence may represent material built up as a result of human occupation, no doubt reduced and of a different type, rather than from complete desertion.

So changed were the functions of the Roman settlement that the street grid was lost for almost half a millennium until c. 900, when perhaps only the High Street re-emerged from the Roman plan, further north on a somewhat different alignment. Thus the city ceased to show clearly the defining features of town life (see p. 23). If the textile *gynaecaeum* closed in AD 407 then this may have been a contributory factor.

The transformation of Roman Winchester may not have been failure but adaptation. The collapse of town life, as it happened, coincided with the sack of Rome in the early fifth century. However, links between outlying provinces and Rome were tenuous by the fifth century; and we must look to local conditions for clarification.

What replaced the Winchester of spacious town houses with their mosaic floors and tiled roofs? The few clues there are can be surprising. First, there was the extension of the occupied area of the city, especially in the west, which had not been occupied before with any intensity – in other words, some change of focus. Second, there is the presence of a new feature in the archaeology: extensive evidence of ironworking. Third, the defences were strengthened in more than one place by the addition of bastions. Fourth, there are significantly enlarged cemeteries surrounding the city. Such evidence can be interpreted variously. It could indicate the weakening of imperial bonds and the development of a new military culture in the shell of the old Roman city; or, alternatively, it could indicate a strengthening of connections with Rome with the added military presence and even the establishment of a Roman diocese based on Winchester, c. AD 350–500. Whatever the driving forces behind changes in the city at this period, structures were more flimsy. It is possible to suggest the extension of town life in Roman Winchester by half a century or so into the early 400s by use of these military and industrial scraps of evidence.

Even so, the arguments for a continuance beyond 400 of 'urban' Winchester are more difficult to sustain, not least because cemetery evidence, our major source for the key indicator – population concentration – diminishes. There seems to be a fifty-year period in the fifth century for which there is remarkably little evidence. Indeed, the rapid dislocation in the pattern, and decline in the number, of burials which had characterized Winchester archaeology throughout the last two centuries of the Roman settlement signals the end of Roman Winchester.

3
Wintanceaster: continuity and invasions
c. 450–1066

Saxon Winchester

In Saxon times the Roman name Venta Belgarum gave way to Wintanceaster. The 'ceaster' element in Old English indicates a place recognized by the Saxons as a Roman walled site – the walls were among those Roman features which pierced the 'dark earth'. The survival of the 'Venta' element in the name indicates contact – of an unknown nature – between Saxons and natives, and hints at continuity in some form from the Roman period. However, no date can be assigned to these contacts between natives and invaders. At the end of the Roman period in Winchester Saxon immigrants came: there is no evidence of Angles or Jutes in the Winchester area. The population of Winchester fell dramatically following the end of Roman Britain: datable material evidence from, for example, cemeteries, falls off, and the archaeologist has thus assumed population decrease.

There is sparse fifth-century pagan Saxon pottery from pits on Lower Brook Street. In the Winchester hinterland, for example at Worthy Park, cemeteries begin in the late fifth century. Such survivals could indicate that Winchester continued as a centre of authority, or even as a focus of deliberate settlement by the Saxons, encouraged by a sub-Roman British authority based on the town. However, a map of fifth- and sixth-century archaeological evidence shows little evidence of occupation within the walled city (see **1**). From present evidence there seems to be a break between Roman and Saxon occupation in the city itself: cemeteries in the surrounding area could relate to settlements outside the walls.

The sixth century

In the sixth century there was military activity associated with either attackers or defenders as exemplified by iron weapons in graves, such as a knife at Winnall and a spearhead from St Giles Hill. Pagan Saxons buried in a concentration of cemeteries outside the walls in the sixth century appear to have been the successors of the British natives. Cemeteries at Winnall east of the city, the first of which has been dated to the sixth or early seventh century, included decapitated burials, such as those found in Roman cemeteries. Such continuity of burial practice could be coincidental, but could, with the discovery of weapons, indicate continuity of military and perhaps administrative urban functions.

Significantly, in this context in the fifth or sixth century the South Gate collapsed but traffic continued over the rubble until the early seventh century when access at that point was cut off by a ditch. Entry to the city from the south could then have been by the undated King's Gate (as it came to be known after the Norman Conquest), which gave access perhaps to the site of a royal palace which remains to be discovered archaeologically (p. 40). Martin Biddle interprets the centre of power as being, as it had been in Roman Winchester, 'a site in or adjacent to the basilica of the forum, just to the west and north of the present cathedral' within 40m (130ft) of the west front of the seventh-century church. This hypothetical royal site, which probably underlies the western part of the medieval graveyard (where the two war memorials now stand outside the west door of the cathedral – it was not found on the Cathedral Visitors' Centre site), could contribute information to the debate about Winchester in the early Saxon period.

The seventh century

At present we cannot be sure of what existed within the walls in the fifth, sixth and early seventh centuries. However, the authority which restricted access to the city at South Gate intended to protect something, but what? A palace and royal centre would seem the only option before the return of Christianity.

A pagan 'princely' burial at Oliver's Battery, south-west of the city, has been dated to the early part of the seventh century and contained a splendid metal hanging bowl, now in the British Museum. This could suggest some form of Saxon authority in the vicinity, perhaps in succession to a residual British authority, if such there was. A further cemetery, Winnall II, of the late seventh or eighth century, sustains the argument for continuity in the environs of the city.

Conversion of the West Saxons to Christianity followed the arrival of the missionary Birinus in 635. Without royal approval Christianity could not take root. A chapel, only 29m (95ft) long, founded in the reign of Cenwalh (642–73), became Old Minster. This may initially have been a royal chapel rather than the seat of a bishop, but reflection on the post-Norman-Conquest text of the *Anglo-Saxon Chronicle*, which suggests 648 as a foundation date for Old Minster, the transfer of the see from Dorchester-on-Thames by Haedda, and the appointment of the first bishop, Wine, in 660, leaves little time – if the dates are right – for the development of an earlier royal chapel.

Archaeology is unlikely to be able to distinguish royal from ecclesiastical work on the Minster site within so narrow a time-frame. It is comparative historical evidence from the Continent which supports the argument for a royal foundation, especially if there was continuity of authority at Winchester from Roman times. The resurgence of Christianity established a religious base which, together with royal status, has remained a key to Winchester's fortunes. Put another way, whereas Romans were buried outside cities, Saxons were increasingly to be buried inside the walls.

Urban estates

Before the relaying of the streets and the creation of the late ninth-century 'burh', at least six estates can be proposed within the town walls from archaeological, topographical and place-name evidence. The royal and ecclesiastical enclosure based on Old Minster and the palace is one, which later in Aethelwold's time (mid-tenth century) became The Close.

Various phases of another compound were excavated at Lower Brook Street. First, a burial dated *c*. 650–700 of a Christian female was found. Her necklace denoted high status (**colour plate 3**) and the aristocratic lady may have been associated with the lord of an early Christian estate on which she and others were buried. Apart from remains of Roman buildings, apparently not in use at the time of the burial, no recognizable structure was found which was contemporary with the burial. Later on the same site there was a structure, unusually of stone, by the ninth century, which produced evidence of gold-working. This building developed into St Mary, Tanner Street, but whether it was from its foundation a church or chapel, or had other functions, has not been determined.

Further enclosures are known from documentary sources: at Coitebury, within the north-eastern sector of the Roman walled area (see **36**); at Wulf's Isle (Wolvesey); New Minster, and the area bounded by Colebrook Street which was given as an endowment to Nunnaminster. A further estate, Godbegot, is discussed below (p. 50).

The early bishop's residence and its estate, from the period before the ninth century, may have been another such compound. The site of this early bishop's palace is predicted by Martin Biddle to have been to the south of Old Minster. Any such structure would be directly beneath the cathedral.

Winchester and Hampshire

As the evidence of territorial organization can be detected in microcosm within the walls of Winchester, so macroscopically it can be seen in the area surrounding the city. In 757 the first reference to Hampshire, the earliest of the shires to be mentioned in a document by name, is found. At first sight, Winchester does not appear to have been central to the establishment of Hampshire, which drew on the name of Hamtun, the settlement at Southampton, to become the 'county of [South]hampton'. This may have referred initially to a Jutish area in the south of the county and the Isle of Wight, perhaps beyond the jurisdiction of the Winchester authority. A centre of power in that area could have been associated with the Roman settlement, Clausentum, on the east bank of the Itchen at Bitterne, which gave way to the thriving town of Saxon [South]hampton, founded c. 700 across the river. Two names are found for this Saxon settlement at Southampton: Hamtun, which implies a royal vill and administrative centre, and Hamwic, which suggests a trading settlement.

This place-name by no means proves the precedence of Southampton. Winchester may well have been a focus for the non-Jutish area north of Southampton. In any case, Saxon kings were itinerant and had a number of residences which they used in succession. So Winchester may have been in Saxon times, as today, the administrative centre of the northern area of Hampshire, with a significant royal and ecclesiastical core. It can be argued that Saxon Winchester, like Southampton, took little account of its Roman predecessor, but as in other counties, for example Dorset (Dorchester) and Gloucestershire (Gloucester), the Roman centres became pre-eminent. The increasing evidence of internal organization, wealth and population growth within Winchester supports this interpretation.

But such matters are not easily resolved. The question of mints is a point at issue. Coins of Egbert (809–39) and Aethelwulf (839–58), for example, have no mint signature so their origin is uncertain. They may have originated at Hamwic, but could have come from Winchester. Unequivocal evidence of a mint in Winchester comes from Alfred's reign (871–99), but the numbers of coins are low, suggesting that minting began at Winchester late in the reign. Mints are not, of course, the only evidence. Pre-Alfredian activity is exemplified in a number of instances and on a number of sites: ironworking (Nunnaminster site) and domestic buildings (The Square and Lower Barracks). Cemetery evidence (Staple Gardens) took the form of some 200 graves possibly of ninth-century date, perhaps, it has been suggested, of immigrants from Southampton after the middle Saxon town was devastated by invaders.

Viking raids

The Vikings attacked Winchester in 860. A Rhenish brooch of the ninth century recovered from the city exemplifies prior links with northern Europe in the age of the Vikings. However, by the reign of Alfred such relations were characterized by warfare as the Vikings attacked inland settlements. In recent years the Vikings have been represented in a more benevolent light than of old. But without doubt they were warriors who galvanized the authorities in Wessex into action.

The defences of Winchester were weak by this time. They were repaired in the first overall restoration since the fourth century. Not surprisingly such a major undertaking took time: references in West Saxon charters to the exaction of fortress-work first appear in the reign of King Aethelbald (855–60). A remarkable correlation has been shown between the length of the defences in the Burghal Hidage (a document of c. 918, in the time of Edward the Elder (899–924) perhaps referring to arrangements made over many years to defend sites against the Vikings) and the known extent of the Roman walls at Winchester.

The existence of ditches from Alfred's time can be shown, but nothing is known of wall-works. For example, upcast, cut by later pits and dated by pottery, from a recut ditch has been excavated to the west of the city (Sussex Street) and a ditch to the north (City Road) of the city from the age of Alfred (see **7**).

A new street grid was laid out as a secondary activity to the refurbishment of the defences. The new system was in essence unitary, although excavation at Staple Gardens appeared to reveal the extension of the grid westwards, and that the grid was established in stages.

This new system did not generally respect the Roman layout. The High Street was on a slightly different alignment east of the West Gate. However, recent analysis of work at The Brooks indicates that there was some correlation with the Roman grid on a north–south street excavated in 1987–8. The Saxon grid contained novel features, such as a street running round the inside of the walls to provide easy access to the defences. Streets such as St Swithun Street, within the southern wall of the city, still respect this Saxon plan. The Saxon town was organized in plots with a regular perch (20m/66ft) between each street.

Two street surfaces excavated in the south-west quarter of the city (Assize Courts South) are assuredly of Saxon date. The first was dated by a coin of Edward the Elder from the early tenth century (1964) and by a coin of Alfred (1990), and the second by a dirham of Samarkand minted in 898. These exciting pre-Norman finds demonstrated that the street plan, although at this point later buried by Norman castle earthworks, was not Roman. The archaeological evidence for the street plan is strengthened by documentary evidence from the foundation charter of New Minster (901) and documented bounds of Nunnaminster written down before 903.

Smaller Saxon 'service' streets lay behind the main thoroughfare, such as those now named St George Street and St Clement Street, but archaeological evidence is not conclusive. Taken together, the evidence suggests a series of works at Winchester lasting well over half a century.

What is certain is that even before the Norman Conquest elements of this plan were obliterated, notably by the creation, probably in the tenth century, of a new Saxon royal palace nearer to the High Street between The Pentice and Market Street, north-east of the early palace site (p. 53; see **28**).

Such work and expenditure adds up to three things. First, this created a 'burh' at Winchester, one of a series of such defended sites deployed across Wessex. Second, it made Winchester 'a town again' in the sense that there was more potential for dense population and heterogeneous urban functions other than those associated with a royal or episcopal vill. Third, the establishment of a new royal palace overriding the new-laid street grid, gave impetus to Winchester's late Saxon role as a capital and royal centre.

Alfred and Edward the Elder

Hamo Thornycroft's mighty statue, erected in 1901, made Alfred's presence in the city tangible. However, Alfred was not a monarch for whom Winchester was a favourite resort. A single visit in 896, when he had Vikings from two raiding ships summarily hanged, is recorded in the *Anglo-Saxon Chronicle*. While this might represent an understatement of his involvement in Winchester, it is all the written evidence we have of his physical presence in the city (**20**).

Alfred's association with the foundation of a navy centred on the south coast may imply that there was some special link between Winchester and Southampton, an obvious base for such a force. Alfred was apparently generous to the city for, as late as the twelfth century, there are references to books, believed to have been the gift of Alfred, which had been in the city for centuries – and which did not survive the destruction and anarchy of Stephen's reign.

Alfred's son, Edward the Elder, showed a firmer commitment to Winchester. Edward strengthened royal status by the foundation of New Minster, a well-endowed religious house which became the burial place for West Saxon kings. On completion of the building works,

20 *Alfred in the neatherd's cottage in Somerset, where he reputedly burnt the cakes, sculpted by Edward Stephens (1860) for the Mansion House, London (photograph: Geremy Butler; copyright: Guildhall Museum and Art Gallery).*

Alfred's body was removed from its place among previous Saxon kings in Old Minster and reburied beside his wife Ealhswith (died 903), creating the long-term link between the great king and the capital of Wessex.

From Edward's reign until the mint was removed (before 1250), the city was a centre for coin production (p. 67). As a royal burial place and with a royal mint and palace, the city's future for the time being was assured.

Saxon economy: trade and industry

The nature of the economic driving force behind Saxon Winchester is not securely identified, but must have been allied to the growing political and religious significance of the city. One element may have been a luxury trade, or development of the wool trade in the middle Saxon period for which there is strong evidence at Hamwic. The wool trade was especially valuable to the economy of Winchester as the religious houses came more and more to rely on the profits from their endowed lands in order to expand.

The building and development of Old Minster from the seventh to the eleventh century represented a long-term local industry, which relied on the supply of materials some of which came from a distance. Any stone, other than local flint or chalk, not reused from Roman remains must have been brought to the city, for example from Coombe Down, near Bath. Limestone fragments were recovered from the robbed-out footing trenches of Old Minster. It appears that the Saxons were using new-quarried Bath stone, both for carved pieces and for other purposes, from the beginnings of work at Old Minster in the middle of the seventh century.

More Coombe Down stone is to be seen in those parts of the cathedral, notably the piers of the south side of the nave, which were built after the demolition of Old Minster, than in the eastern arm. This could strengthen the argument that the lower courses of the nave were built out of Bath stone from Old Minster, and would explain the wholesale robbing of stone from the Saxon minster.

Trade, industry and administrative activity require adequate communications. The middle of the ninth century – 859 – is the traditional date assigned to the rebridging of the Itchen under Swithun (see pp. 46–50). Swithun's bridge, now rebuilt as the City Bridge near the site of East Gate, no doubt replaced a lost Roman bridge. The re-establishment of Winchester as a bridging point was significant economically and may have contributed to the subsequent popularity of Swithun as a local saint.

The growing economy led to the expansion of suburbs to accommodate the work-force. Tenth-century material remains include evidence of a thriving western suburb, beyond the defended 'burh' and adjacent to the old Iron Age defences (Carfax and Sussex Street). One of this suburb's numerous latrine pits produced a remarkable saint's reliquary (**21**). In the decade before 1066, practitioners of trades were concentrated in particular streets identified by their occupational names (p. 50)

Three minsters

Winchester's significance as a religious centre gathered momentum in the centuries following the foundation of Old Minster, which was joined after 900 by New Minster and Nunnaminster. New Minster was placed on land bought with gold by Edward the Elder. It may have been created as a burial place for his father, Alfred. However, its spacious proportions (790sq m/8504sq ft; compare 354sq m/3810sq ft for Old Minster at this time) suggest a place of worship for the people. Like Old Minster in the tenth century it was staffed by secular clerks.

Nunnaminster, founded adjacent to Old and New Minsters, provided an opportunity for holy women to practise their faith within a cloister. Remains of the church, uncovered by excavations, are displayed in Abbey Passage beside the Guildhall. Nunnaminster was built on land which belonged to Alfred's Mercian wife, Ealhswith (died 903): its boundaries were written into a prayer book of c. 900, whose Mercian origins link it to Ealhswith. Edward the Elder's daughter

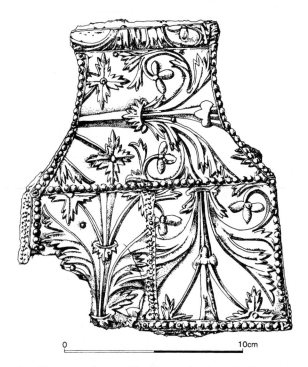

21 *Fragment of a portable silver on beechwood reliquary recovered from a tenth-century latrine pit in the wealthy western suburb (Sussex Street, 1976) (after Nigel Fradgley; redrawn by Philip Marter).*

Eadburh, who was later beatified, entered Nunnaminster as an infant; excavations there have uncovered what appear to be remains of a shrine to this local West Saxon saint (see **57**).

These three great churches have been partly excavated and researched by the Winchester Research Unit and the Winchester Museums Archaeology Section. The most extensive excavations were at Old Minster in the 1960s. As a result, the outlines of Old Minster are now marked out, and a complex series of phases of development is explained by information boards, north-west of the cathedral (**22**). In addition, a computer model has been produced in which the viewer can enjoy a video simulation of both interior and exterior views of this great church, exploring the sight-lines of the kings from their seats at the west end. Associated finds have thrown light on its structure and decor, which in later phases included glazed pottery and relief-tiles used as borders for important areas, and

22 *Plan of Old Minster laid out beside the nave of the present cathedral. The seventh-century rectangular structure (below, **23**a) is outlined in bricks (centre). The location of Swithun's tomb is seen (top), where the cathedral nave and the minster plan converge (below, **23**c) (photograph: John Crook).*

blue window glass, some fragments perhaps dating back to the seventh-century church.

High-status works at the minsters – decoration such as mural painting, and fittings such as the organ in New Minster which is illustrated in a manuscript – are matched by the quality of the architecture, such as the magnificent westworks of Old Minster and New Minster (see **25**). There seems no reason to doubt that Nunnaminster was also a splendid structure.

Tenth-century reform

A mixture of local, national and international considerations strengthened religious developments in the tenth century. The international component was the reformation of religious communities in western Christendom after 950. In Wessex this was achieved, not without serious opposition, by King Edgar and Bishop Aethelwold, who was appointed by the king in 963. Aethelwold was born in Winchester and is the first named person known to have been born in the city.

The reforms took concrete form in Winchester with the replacement by monks of the clerks at Old and New Minsters, and with the reform of Nunnaminster. Benefits flowed from this change: not least that the communal monks were much more cost-effective than the clerks they replaced, and so they were thought to be a better investment and thus more pleasing to God, which encouraged benefactors to give.

King Edgar led the way in endowing the monastery. He returned three major estates at Taunton (Somerset), Downton (Wiltshire) and Alresford (Hampshire) together with five other manors to Bishop Aethelwold, in all some 500 hides. Landed income and gifts enabled the building of the startling structures of the rebuilt Old Minster. Ecclesiastical Winchester influenced the Old English kingdom right up to the Norman Conquest.

So it was that King Edgar and Bishop Aethelwold laid the foundations of the wealth of the Winchester diocese. The lands which passed from Edgar to Aethelwold formed the basis of the income which made Winchester the wealthiest see in England throughout the Middle Ages, wealthier even than the archbishopric of Canterbury, which Winchester was to challenge for the right to be an archiepiscopal see.

The substitution of monks for clerks at the minsters, coupled with the generosity to the bishop by Edgar, was at the expense of dispossessed men of substance: high-born clerks and lay thegns. Some lost their manors in the endowment of the minster, other lay people had their houses demolished in the settling of boundaries between Old and New Minsters. Such tensions may have contributed to the murder of Edward the Martyr in Wessex in 978, and to continuing instability in Wessex through to 1066.

Swithun

Political instability fuelled a continuing growth in Church power. A final element in the reordering of religious life and experience in Winchester came in 971 with the revelation of the ninth-century bishop Swithun's powers through a series of miracles. In 974 the saint's remains were relocated in pride of place in the new buildings of Old Minster. Wulfstan Cantor, an eyewitness, recorded that it poured with rain during the ceremony, which is thought to be the origin of the saying which relates rain on Swithun's day to rain for forty days afterwards.

The discovery and/or rediscovery of saints' remains was an especially English feature of tenth-century reformed monasticism. Also, New Minster already boasted the remains of Alfred and of other kings at this time. The question must be asked: why was Swithun selected as patron of Winchester? Why not Birinus, apostle of Wessex; Haedda, who had translated the see to Winchester; or Beornstan, whose sanctity was the subject of a special revelation to Aethelwold?

One answer is rather disappointing. According to Wulfstan, Swithun was chosen because there was general ignorance of him. In some respects ignorance persists, for example Swithun's death occured in the period 861 to 863, we do not know precisely when. This uncertainty is

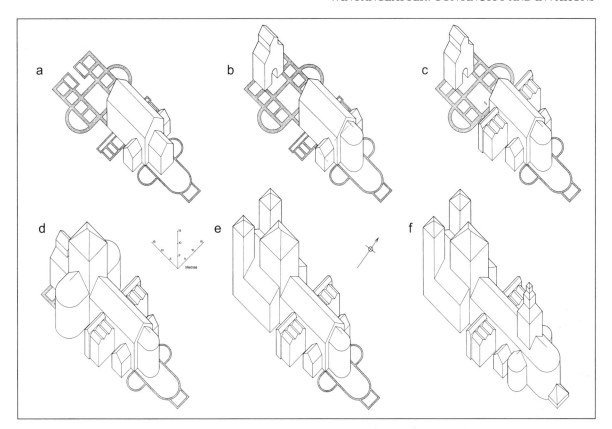

23 *Old Minster: structural development,* c. 648 *to* c. *993–4. The seventh-century chapel developed westwards, to incorporate the tomb of Swithun which became a shrine (copyright: Winchester Research Unit).*

expressed in citing the date as 861x3. Excavation has shown that Swithun's burial was just outside the original western entrance of Old Minster, as can be deduced from the reconstruction of Old Minster's ruins (**23**). Because Swithun was there, the area became a precinct reserved for 'the noble and distinguished'. It can thus be argued that Wulfstan was being disingenuous. Swithun must surely have been known to the monks of Old Minster.

It is perhaps plausible to suggest that Swithun was 'promoted' a century after his death because a re-evaluation of his life had much to commend it. Swithun had not been a monk as the occupants of the reformed minsters were. He had been one of those clerks who had been rejected in the Aethelwoldian reforms. It is most likely that he belonged to the class excluded by Aethelwold. His resuscitation therefore had all sorts of potential benefits. He was local, saintly and non-monastic, so he could be paraded to bridge the gap between the reformed monks and the more substantial

clerks who had preceded them in the minster. Last but not least, Swithun was remembered as having the common touch, as revealed in the miracle at East Gate where he saved the eggs (**24**). The beatification of Swithun was by no means a fraud but it does have the hallmarks of necessity being the mother of invention.

By 980 the protagonists were changing. Aethelwold's reforms had been carried through with royal support. Now he could repay the compliment to King Ethelred, who had been hastily thrust into prominence by his half-brother Edward's murder in 978. The occasion which brought these threads together was the rededication of Old Minster on 20 October 980.

Various elements were united by this important event in the city's history. The monastic

24 *The miracle in which Swithun (left) restores the broken eggs of a poor woman who fell as she was crossing the bridge on her way to market (Corhampton church, photograph: John Crook).*

direction in which the reformed minster had been set by Aethelwold was confirmed. Continuing royal interest was reflected in the ceremonial westwork of the new building, which has been shown to have continental parallels, especially in Germany. Inside the building Ethelred processed to a special throne to receive ecclesiastical blessing. This ceremony was undoubtedly significant in reinforcing Winchester's royal and ecclesiastical pre-eminence in Wessex.

At about this time, the date is not precisely known but was probably before 980, the bishop's complex at Wolvesey was created, replacing that which is believed to lie beneath the present cathedral. Wolvesey probably included a hall (which continued in use until the early twelfth century) and residential accommodation. There was also a curious oval structure which may have been a chapel, a structure matched to the north of the cathedral on the Wessex Hotel site, formerly the New Minster cemetery. The development of Wolvesey completed the occupation of the southeast quarter of the city by rich ecclesiastical buildings.

Late Saxon triumph

The last two centuries of Saxon Winchester, which ended with the Norman Conquest in 1066, were dominated by building at the minsters

25 Reconstructions of New Minster (left) and the westworks of Old Minster, covering Swithun's tomb, from the north-west, in their most magnificent state c. 993–4 to 1093 (copyright: Winchester Research Unit).

(**25**). Provision of masonry, window-glass, bells and the famous organ all support this picture. An early eleventh-century carved ivory panel from a book, found at St Cross, and now in the City Museum, is a fine example of Winchester art of a late Saxon date and can be compared with figure drawings in contemporary illuminated manuscripts. Metalwork and ivory found in excavations are sufficient to constitute the output of a Winchester School of manuscript and plastic arts. These objects are mirrored in church wall painting such as that found at Nether Wallop.

All this demonstrates the high status of late Saxon Winchester. Compared with the local grass-tempered ware characteristic of the local economy up to the eighth century, 'sandy ware' and 'Winchester ware' are now found. Winchester ware is wheel-made pottery of high quality, but was not widely distributed beyond Winchester (**26**). The Brooks excavation of 1987–8 produced thousands of fragments of apparently Saxon glass. These finds were highly unusual both in their quantity, manufacture and their context, and matched material from Old Minster. The discovery of two Byzantine lead seals, a silver-gilt repoussé head (that is, beaten into relief from the inside) and an Egyptian alabaster vessel in late Saxon layers, leave no doubt about the extended links of the populous and flourishing city at the end of the Saxon period.

The period of rather less than a century which separates the rededication of Old Minster from the Norman Conquest and the beginnings of the new cathedral, was the high point in Winchester's development as a capital city. Successive kings paid homage to the city. Some, such as Cnut (died 1035), were buried there. Scandinavian influence comes to the fore from his reign, as exemplified in the Gunni tombstone and a Scandinavian rune-stone found in the city (**27**).

The Church continued to benefit from its symbiotic relationship with the crown. The estate north of the High Street, which was known as Godbegot, a name preserved today for the fine courtyard house on part of the estate, was given to Queen Emma by Ethelred II in 1012. On her death it was bequeathed to the cathedral priory and remained its property until 1541. The estate in Saxon times was more extensive than it was in later periods, and included a 'fair church' erected by a prefect of the city named Ethelwine, and dedicated to St Peter. Remains of this church were excavated in the 1950s when a stone chancel was discovered (now marked on the paving in St George Street), but no evidence of a nave was found by excavation. There were numbers of other Saxon churches in Winchester, such as St Mary in Tanner Street. and Saxon gate-churches at exits from the city.

The largest landowners were, on retrospective evidence found in the twelfth-century Winton Domesday, the bishop, the prior, the abbot of New Minster and the abbess of St Mary (Nunnaminster). The king was lord of the whole borough and was rewarded with ground-rent (landgable). The city's architectural and artistic heritage and archaeology at this period show that it enjoyed an impressively broad range of activities, including clothworking, tanning and metalworking, which mark out significant urban communities from their lesser counterparts.

Optimism arising from lay and ecclesiastical reconciliation at the rededication of Old Minster in 980 was apparently well founded. None the less little over a century later Old Minster was to be sacrificed by the Normans to their mighty cathedral church. Although the Normans adopted many of the Saxons' best practices (for example the monastic organization at the minster/cathedral), they destroyed the Saxon royal line and Old Minster which had existed for over 400 years. Along with the minsters, the buildings of Saxon Winchester have been obliterated by succeeding generations, but much of the Saxon street system still survives and with it numbers of individual house plots and certain urban estates and place-names.

Analysis of the population of late Saxon Winchester buttresses understanding of the

26 *A Winchester ware glazed pottery vessel, ht. 25.3cm (10in), rim diameter 12cm (5in), excavated at The Brooks in 1987–8. This pottery is found from c. 950 up to the twelfth century (photograph: John Crook; copyright: Winchester City Museums).*

significance of Saxon Winchester. Retrospective material in twelfth-century surveys reveals that the population of Winchester in *c.* 1057 (dated by the names of moneyers living in the city at that date) lived in 1130 tenements and may have numbered 5500. A higher figure of 8000 is implied by a different method of calculation. The figure of 8000 represents a population of Winchester larger than any between the Black Death of 1348 and the 1820s. This evidence is confirmed by mint evidence which places Winchester perhaps fourth in England after London, York and Lincoln.

A unique insight into Winchester society before the Norman Conquest is provided by an unparalleled study of personal names found in a survey *c.* 1057. Most names were native Old English: at least 50 per cent and perhaps over 75 per cent. Between 5 and 10 per cent are continental Germanic, perhaps representing immigrants who had participated in the Norman invasion, from places like Lotharingia in northern Europe. In addition, there is a small but significant number of Scandinavian names representing two

27 *A rare Scandinavian burial at the Cathedral Green, perhaps from the time of Cnut (died 1035), of a man aged approximately 23. The inscription translates: 'Here lies G[un]n[i], Eorl's [or the earl's] fellow.' Note the hand-of-God footstone (copyright: Winchester Research Unit).*

groups: Scandinavians who had migrated to Normandy (giving the area its name) and direct migrants from Scandinavia from the time of Cnut.

The end of Saxon England and the eclipse of its capital were as swift as they were surprising. Signs of the increasing importance of London as a royal centre were already visible from the reign of Ethelred II (978–1016), who, significantly, was buried in St Paul's, although his successors Cnut (died 1035) and Harthacnut (1040–2) chose to be buried at Winchester. However, the remarkable excavations of the minsters, the painstaking re-evaluation of Viking and Saxon activities and rulers, and the recognition of Saxon pottery, metalwork, art and architecture combine today to give substance to the established tradition which described Saxon Winchester thriving as 'the ancient capital of England'.

4

Norman Winchester

1066–1150

Conquest

By the end of 1066 Winchester's fate was sealed, for on Christmas Day 1066 William the Conqueror was crowned king not in Wessex but at Westminster. There Edward the Confessor, whose heir William claimed to be, had begun his abbey *c.* 1050, and there Edward was buried. Succession was settled at Hastings in October 1066. Winchester acceded gracefully to Duke William in November and opened its gates. Had Winchester closed its gates to him it is uncertain whether he could have conquered it. He certainly could not have taken London.

A rebellion in 1069 drew William's attention to Stigand, Bishop of Winchester, whose family was allegedly involved. At the Easter Council at Winchester in 1070 Stigand was removed both as Bishop of Winchester and as Archbishop of Canterbury. This cleared the way for a new ecclesiastical start in the city and diocese. Great building activities at the castle and palace had already begun to transform the city by 1072, when the castle provided a useful prison for Stigand.

Also in 1072 King William's new chapel at the castle was the scene of meetings to discuss the issue of the primacy of Canterbury and York as archiepiscopal sees. It is perhaps significant that such a meeting was held in Winchester, on neutral ground so far as the archbishops were concerned. However, it was a meeting at the initiative of the king, and not one which was in the domain of the clergy at the minsters.

Castle and royal palace

The Norman invasion was not purely destructive; at first the Normans enlarged and extended the types of structures which the Saxons had created, such as minsters and a palace. Winchester had a part to play in Norman England, but never as its capital: William I governed as he moved around the country.

Winchester was controlled from a castle built on the western side of the valley, within the Roman circuit of defences, south of the West Gate. This hillside position dominated the city which spread east of the castle down towards the Itchen. The Winchester keep of this early date has not been found by excavation. However, the king was secure at Winchester and the treasury remained in the city. Arrangements at Winchester where a royal palace lay beside the cathedral monastery mirrored those being set in place in London at the same time where a residence was developed beside the monastic complex at Westminster.

In the south-western salient of the defences, over four dozen stone and timber houses were demolished or buried in the creation of the castle platform. This artificially levelled-up site surmounted by a Norman keep must have been tremendously impressive. Today, although the keep has long gone, the great flight of steps which runs up beside the law courts to the medieval Great Hall of the castle gives an impression of the enormous earthworks which the construction of a castle platform in that location

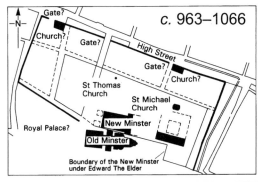

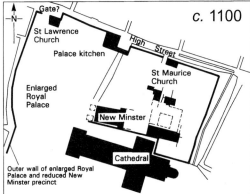

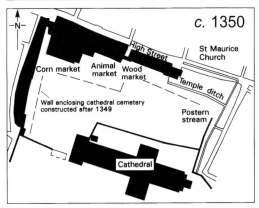

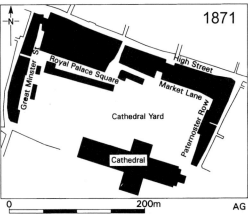

28 *Plans of the late Saxon and Norman palace site. The site of the Norman kitchen (the square structure centre top c. 1100) is known from documentary sources of c. 1100 and c. 1350. The palace buildings lay west of the kitchen under what is now The Pentice and included the site of St Lawrence church (after Keene and OS: drawn by Alejandra Gutierrez).*

demanded. At the northern end of this platform a mighty mound of earth was created, revetted by a stone wall, to dominate the western entrance of the city. A keep was created, together with its accompanying buildings.

A royal chapel within the castle enclosure, perhaps the location of the archbishops' meeting of 1072, has been excavated. It was constructed with long-and-short-work quoins characteristic of Saxon building technique (not found in the cathedral begun in 1079). The internal plaster contained crushed tile to give a pink colour similar to the interior of Old Minster. As the chapel ignores the Saxon street plan, which had been buried at that point, it must be part of the Norman castle works.

The Saxon palace (p. 42; **28**) adjacent to the northern boundaries of the religious houses, was extended by the Normans. Royal visitors stayed in the palace, which documentary evidence suggests doubled in size around 1070, although there is as yet virtually no archaeological evidence of it, other than a wall excavated in the vicinity of St Lawrence church. The rebuilt palace was splendid, 'second neither in design nor size to those at London'. Kitchens are referred to on a site now immediately adjacent to the eastern end of The Pentice, south of the High Street, where twelve houses were destroyed to make room for them (see **28**). Today, the projection of structures on the corner of Market Street into the High Street ghost the site of the kitchen (**29**). William also built a hall and other palace buildings.

These major works, together with those at the cathedral (below), may have encouraged some of the overseas links of late eleventh-century Winchester, which are found in the archaeological record: four Byzantine coins and seals, and, more prosaically, Andenne pottery from Belgium.

29 *25 High Street, formerly Ratners, projects into the High Street echoing the encroachment of the royal kitchen into the High Street (photograph: John Crook).*

Around 1100 the castle began to combine the functions of residence and fortress, perhaps at the expense of the palace. The castle remained a major treasure house in the reign of Henry I (1100–35), who rode there to secure his treasure on the death of his brother, William II (Rufus).

Winchester Cathedral and Nunnaminster

It was in a city already witnessing two major building projects, at the castle and the palace, that work on the cathedral was begun in 1079–80 (**colour plate 4**). By this time the realm was secure and the ecclesiastical hierarchy had been reorganized (p. 52). The capital of the Saxon kings was appropriate for a new, grand building of 'colonial' proportions to leave no doubt that in ecclesiastical matters as in lay, the Saxon age was finished.

On 8 April 1093, fourteen years after it was begun, the formal dedication of the east end of the new cathedral took place. The remains of Swithun were removed from Old Minster and set in the eastern arm of the new building in a surprising enthusiasm for a Saxon saint by conquerors generally sceptical of the sanctity of those revered by people they had conquered.

Materials for facing the new cathedral had to be brought from a distance: mainly quarries at Binstead, near Ryde, on the Isle of Wight. The very considerable amounts of material used in the walls faced by this ashlar were local flints. This building, the longest of its kind in Europe at that date, was intended to impress. To imagine Winchester with its Norman castle, palace and cathedral gives a clear impression of Church and State in the later eleventh century.

But a view of Winchester with all these projects completed at once would be illusory, because the plans evolved as time passed (**30**), and because different elements were in train at different times. The spectacular length of the cathedral nave is a puzzle, and was late on the scene. The Conqueror had respected Winchester, and his son Rufus supported the cathedral with additional grants of quarry-land in the Isle of Wight. However, the restless life-style of William I, visiting lands in France and England, and the predilection of Rufus for court and hunting meant Winchester Cathedral was increasingly a project which had to take its chance. Bishop Walkelin (1070–98) was undoubtedly an ideal choice to set the cathedral and diocese on a new track after the pluralistic Stigand.

Nunnaminster was also reordered by the Normans. The dedication to St Eadburh was changed soon after 1066. Excavation has revealed through the alternate plain and complex

30 The Norman cathedral as projected. The westworks were built, but were demolished c. 1350; towers at the corners of the transepts were projected, but internal architecture now shows that the plans changed before they were built (after John Crook; redrawn by Judith Dobie).

arrangement of the pier bases, together with the wide bands of mortar found in Walkelin's work on the cathedral, that the reworking of Nunnaminster was well in hand by *c.* 1100.

Decline in royal status

Rufus (William II, 1087–1100) was not a king whose life recommended him to bishops. Where Rufus had no children and perhaps had an interest in men, Henry I had possibly two dozen illegitimate children by a variety of mistresses. Perchance the private lives, nepotism and patronage of these two kings contributed in some way to the division of Church from State at Winchester.

The cathedral tower collapsed in 1107, seven years after Rufus was buried there, the last king to be so (see **32**). This collapse may have contributed to Henry I's break with Norman tradition *c.* 1110, when he abandoned the Easter crown-wearing at Winchester. The ceremony had become a feature of Norman kingship, presumably since suitable westworks had been completed at the cathedral, if that was where it

took place. Such a tradition was not of long standing, and was easily discarded. The growing influence of London was another significant weight in the balance.

Also around 1110 King Henry initiated a survey of Winchester, possibly an updating of the now-lost 1086 Domesday, to try to discover, as his father had done, what encroachments had occurred on royal estates in the city since the time of Edward the Confessor. It would seem unlikely that such a survey would prove popular, and there is evidence of wary answers from the 86 jurors such as, 'we know not by whom'. Perhaps a symptom of the collapse in Henry's relations with Winchester can be detected in 1118 when one of his treasury staff, Henry the Camerarius, was blinded and castrated for irregularities in treasury affairs. Although the city remained a treasury town thereafter, it was increasingly less significant in that role.

However, relations between Henry I and the city were not always poor. He acted as go-between in the acquisition of lands for New Minster when it moved north of the city to Hyde *c.* 1110. He continued to take an interest for the following two years at least, acting probably on Bishop Giffard's advice.

The survey of *c.* 1110 provides an unrivalled snapshot of the city within half a century of the Conquest. So far as the boundaries of twelfth-century urban Winchester are known they may have been defined by five churches: Winnall (north), St Anastasius (north-west), St James (west), St Giles (east) and St Faith (south). The area of the constituent parts of the city by the late twelfth century, and by analogy also early in the century, consisted of the walled city of 58ha (144 acres) with a somewhat smaller area of 49ha (122 acres) to the south outside the walls, and three roughly equal suburban areas on the north, east and west, each around 20ha (50 acres). Around the expanded city a substantial outer series of defences was begun. These lay outside West Gate and parallel to the ancient defences (**31** and see **36**). The northern section may be seen at Clifton Road. These major works of the early twelfth century were abandoned before completion. The creation and abandonment of such defences may signal shifts of royal interest in Winchester. The 1110 survey thus reveals the city at the height of its medieval development, with a great building programme and a burgeoning population.

Population

From perhaps 8000 before the Conquest, the population may have declined in the turmoil immediately after 1066. But in the early twelfth century the city contained perhaps 1300 houses, making it second to London and larger than both Norwich (1270 houses) and York (1181 houses).

Such figures translate into a population of 8–11,000 in the early twelfth century. At the time of the Winton Domesday of 1148, the city population was probably somewhat diminished as a result of civil war. Because of the widespread destruction chronicled in 1141, a figure nearer 8000 might be appropriate for 1148.

Physical changes in the city are clearly mirrored in the changes in composition of the population. Only 30 per cent of those recorded at Winchester in 1110 had native names, compared with 70 per cent in the pre-Conquest survey. While there was a tendency for those with Norman names to be the more substantial citizens who had gained from the invasion, and so to be recorded, the tilt in balance of power in the city is striking. In addition, there may have been an especial rise in the number of Normans who settled in the royal fief, perhaps one-quarter of the city, to which the survey is restricted. There is, however, no conclusive evidence that the Normans settled in a single area of the city.

Bishops Giffard and Blois: Wolvesey

At first any incipient decline was masked by the building activities of two great bishops: William Giffard (1100–29) and Henry of Blois (1129–71). As Rufus's chancellor, Giffard had been responsible for the cavernous Westminster Hall and was an ideal person to oversee the reconstruction of the collapsed tower and the damaged transepts at Winchester, where the superlative quality, closely

31 *St Mary by West Gate chancel arch, now demolished, and West Gate. The position of the twelfth-century arch shows that the chancel must have pierced the city wall, with the nave outside the wall. This suggests the church was built at the time that the outer defences were in progress (see* **36***)(Author's collection).*

mortared, late Romanesque stonework has Giffard's stamp upon it (**32**).

The creation of the bishop's palace at Wolvesey as probably the greatest Romanesque house in England was accomplished during the episcopates of Giffard, who undoubtedly built the West Hall and range, and of Henry of Blois, who built a great East Hall and much else – although it remains possible that Giffard was the originator of both East and West Halls at Wolvesey (**colour plate 5**).

Among the many architectural features of Wolvesey was a water system, which has been traced in the courtyard and under the south range. Its contents enabled the pottery sequence for Winchester to be re-evaluated and types previously dated to the thirteenth century to be moved firmly into the first half of the twelfth century. Wolvesey also reveals much exceptional high-status building work of the twelfth century as exemplified by the fine stonework of the West Hall, which matches the close-mortared late Romanesque work of the rebuilt cathedral tower. The West Hall enjoyed a raised *piano nobile* overlooking a terraced garden from which the cathedral monastery could be viewed. Much of Giffard's work is now buried beneath the Baroque palace, but the ruins of the northern end of the west range can be seen.

Giffard's successor, Henry of Blois, began his episcopate with major building programmes: the complex at Wolvesey was developed magnificently. The impressive ruins which remain today date largely from the twelfth century. A major consolidation programme was undertaken by the

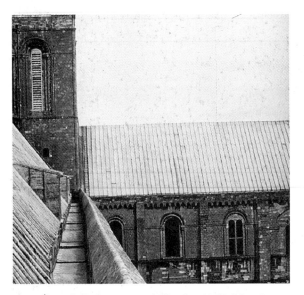

custodian, English Heritage, to display the halls, kitchens and many associated buildings. Embellishments, such as fragments of the ornate Caen stone decoration of the doorway of the west range added by Bishop Henry, are in the City Museum (**33**).

The mid-1130s were notable for another, now largely vanished, building project initiated by Henry of Blois. This was the Hospital of St Cross, with an impressive Romanesque church, parts of which still survive, and a range of ancillary buildings to the south, today seen as earthworks in the meadows (**34**). The now lost

32 *The cathedral tower as rebuilt after 1107. Note the thick mortar of the early work (right) and the fine ashlar of the subsequent early twelfth-century work (centre and in the tower) (photograph: Martin Doughty).*

33 *Caen stone sculpture fragment from Henry of Blois's Wolvesey c. 1140–50, perhaps from a richly decorated doorway. Ht. 15.5cm (6in). Originally polychrome (red eye, black eyebrow and hair) and from a high setting as the top of the head remained uncarved (copyright: Winchester Research Unit).*

34 *St Cross church from the south-east to show twelfth-century work. Originally the hospital buildings lay south of the church (left), and the south side of the church is for that reason somewhat more plain than the north 'public' side (photograph: John Crook).*

35 *The leper hospital of St Mary Magdalen: site plan and aspects of the buildings. The church was rebuilt in the fourteenth century, but the twelfth-century pillars were preserved. It was demolished in the late eighteenth century (Author's collection).*

leper hospital of St Mary Magdalen, east of the city, is another project attributed to Bishop Henry. Romanesque work was still upstanding in the late eighteenth century (**35**). Surprisingly, field walking in the 1980s produced no twelfth-century artefacts.

Civil war and anarchy

The royal palace appears to have ceased to function by the death of Henry I in 1135. Stephen (1135–54), if he stayed at Winchester, probably used the castle, where the treasure was stored. Stephen's reign was very unsettled and, from the city's point of view, crucial. In February 1141 Stephen was captured at Lincoln by forces loyal to his rival, the Empress Matilda. His brother, Henry of Blois, Bishop of Winchester, no doubt sensing disaster for himself in the wake of Stephen's defeat, handed over both crown and treasure to Matilda at Winchester Castle. This turned out to be a false move for the bishop and was almost fatal for Winchester.

Henry of Blois and Matilda came to blows. Matilda was based in the castle and Henry in the old royal palace in the centre of Winchester (or possibly at Wolvesey). In the succeeding battle, areas of the city were devastated and the royal palace destroyed. Although Henry was successful, the price for the city was very high for in August and September 1141 Winchester was burnt – some said torched. Apart from the loss of the royal palace, the castle was attacked on all sides, including from within the city from the Southgate Street area. Quite what the effect on the castle was can only be imagined, but we hear nothing more of it in the remainder of Stephen's reign. To date, little archaeological evidence has been found to endorse the chroniclers' description of the burning of Winchester, although fire damage of the mid-twelfth century, to the south-western part of St Mary's abbey cloister, was uncovered by excavation in 1973.

The 1148 survey

Henry of Blois was responsible for a survey of lands at Winchester in 1148. The survey reveals the city damaged by the civil war (**36**). It is a fuller survey than that of 1110 – perhaps because the bishop was enjoying the benefits not only of his own properties as bishop, but also those of his brother, the king.

36 *Winchester in 1148. Much of the Saxon street plan is clearly seen and the gates are identified. Water courses in Upper Brook Street (Sildwortenestret), Middle Brook Street (Wunegrestret) and Tannerestret, may have contributed to the stabilizing of the water-table by the tenth century, which allowed the creation of a dry crypt for the cathedral. Many of the fifty or so churches of medieval Winchester are located on this map. Castle, cathedral and Wolvesey Palace are seen in their Romanesque plan. The massive earth outer defences to the west of the city, never completed, are noteworthy (after Winchester Research Unit; redrawn by Alejandra Gutierrez).*

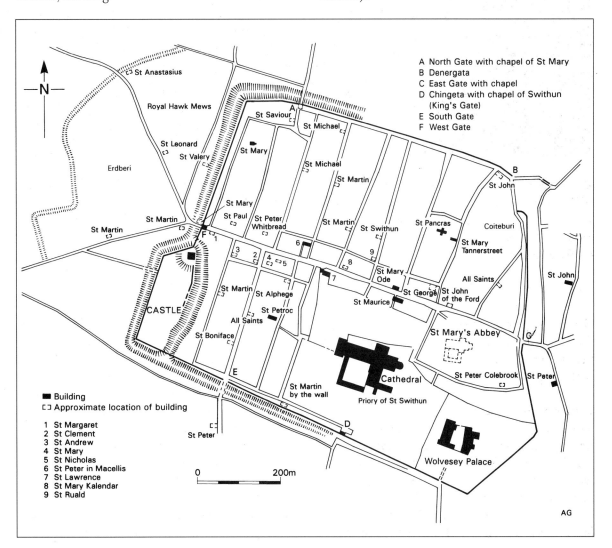

The survey suggests a population of approximately 8000 people occupying 1100 houses. Three suburbs, although not that on the east, were heavily populated. The defensive work begun for the western suburb earlier in the century perhaps encouraged the spread of houses into the suburbs. Within the walls the city was well packed with houses, including the High Street frontage of the defunct royal palace where fifteen tenements had sprung up since 1141. There were high values attached to properties on the main thoroughfares leading to the gates and elsewhere.

Occupations were varied. Royal officials and moneyers dominated town society, but they were neither as numerous nor as important individually as they had been forty years earlier. The moneyers remained in the High Street where they had been since before the Conquest, and were joined in the city by both Christian and Jewish goldsmiths and moneylenders. Otherwise, food trades were common while shoemakers and tanners were dispersing from the streets which bore their names.

Winchester must have shared in the general expansion of European trade which culminated in the commercial revolution of the later twelfth century. Certainly the St Giles Fair, held from the twelfth century on the downs east of the city, continued to expand into the thirteenth century. Set against this speculation, archaeological evidence in the city for outside connections is sparse in the middle and later part of the twelfth century.

Parish churches

The study of parish churches provides a barometer of the fortunes of the city in the Middle Ages: their number and development hint at general trends of boom or decline. Within the city the number of parish churches peaked at some 57 by 1148 (see **36**). Thereafter reduced numbers were probably due to the decline of the city and to developments which flowed from the investiture contest of the eleventh and early twelfth centuries. In this battle of Church and State the Church discouraged lay people from developing private churches, the origin of many of the churches in Winchester. When Salisbury was founded after 1220, it had just three churches – facilitating administration, and with much larger and so more viable parishes than those at Winchester, which were estimated at the height of the churches boom to have covered no more than 1.1ha (2.8 acres) per parish. The clergy formed the largest occupational group at Winchester in 1148. While their buildings no doubt needed maintenance, the unproductive nature of clerkly life boded ill for the future economy of the city.

Evidence of parish churches taken with other materials from the 1148 survey suggests that Winchester may have been maintaining a position among the top six cities of England towards the end of Stephen's reign, but it is difficult to be certain.

Summing up, there is more documentary evidence than for earlier periods, and it tells us much. On the archaeological side there is a comparative dearth at present of domestic material and we have no published pottery sequence, although much evidence survives from the great buildings – cathedral, castle and Wolvesey Palace. The first stone domestic accommodation of the townspeople begins to survive aboveground, notably at 24 St Thomas Street where an early twelfth-century hall survives over a two-bayed undercroft. Like two other such properties known from the city at the time, it was set back from the street. At the other end of the archaeological scale, among the novelties in the archaeological record at this period, are flutes made from goose bone, and small bells from clothing or for undefined ecclesiastical functions.

5

Recovery

1150–1300

A visitor to Winchester in 1150 would have found the city considerably damaged by the siege of 1141. None the less, the principal structure on the skyline would have been the cathedral, and beside it the Norman royal palace, probably in ruins. Wolvesey would have been approaching its fullest Romanesque extent, and at the castle there was the Norman keep. These structures dominated the southern half and margins of the city. Winchester was still under the direction of royal and ecclesiastical authorities, which commanded significant spaces as owners, occupiers or landlords.

This period saw the city flourishing in an age of general economic growth, which is reflected in a variety of ways: in the number of parish churches, the introduction of new religious houses, the friaries, while art and architecture on the grandest scale is plainly seen. On a lesser scale, but still complex, the earliest dated timber-framed house in the city dates from before 1300. The city government developed through grants and charters, and became a property holder in its own right. This was to be significant for the future.

In the city centre, and to the north of the High Street, were the main residential areas. These were served by some fifty parish churches, many of stone, while the housing was predominantly timber-framed on dwarf walls, with a small proportion of high-status stone houses interspersed. Certain streets, for example in the Brooks, were areas of industrial activity, notably textile working. The suburbs were growing.

Henry of Blois: St Cross and the Winchester Bible

Although Bishop Henry left England on Henry II's accession in 1154, he was back in 1158 and developed his buildings until his death in 1171. These architectural works share a number of characteristics among which is the use of significant amounts of Purbeck marble. Bishop Henry's interest in Classical antiquity had already led him to Rome whence he had shipped back *spolia* (see Glossary). It may have been that this excited his interest in marble and led him to seek out suitable materials in England.

Henry of Blois was an innovator in the use of Purbeck marble as his works pre-dated by thirty years or more the 1174 rebuilding of Canterbury Cathedral, a first date commonly given for extensive use of that material. Hyde Abbey and Bishop's Waltham Palace, as well as Wolvesey and St Cross, display carved Purbeck.

At St Cross there was an early unsuccessful experiment in the chancel of the chapel to make Purbeck load-bearing. The black Purbeck column bases can still be seen protruding below casing-columns of limestone. The squared east end of St Cross, in the English style, was a significant triumph. The finely carved late Romanesque decoration of the chancel, both inside and out, is the best of this date in the city.

Henry of Blois made no obvious contribution to the fabric of Winchester Cathedral, apart from the provision of the marble font, from Tournai. His greatest contribution to the cathedral was of another kind: the Winchester Bible (**colour plate 6**). This extraordinary book, among the greatest achievements of twelfth-century art in England, is displayed in the cathedral library. Monumental in concept, the illumination, like the cathedral priory which housed it, was never finished. However, a text was completed, originally bound in two great volumes: each spread measures 583 by 792mm (23 by 31z\v in). A fact revealing about the scale of the Bible is that it took the skins of some 250 calves to create the pages. The decorative lettering was achieved by artists whose contributions can be identified and collated. The decoration of the pages contains much gold leaf, but it is the deep blue lapis lazuli fetched from Afghanistan, more valuable than gold, and of which many times greater quantities were used, that demonstrates the sumptuous nature of the Winchester Bible.

The Bible, associated documents, wall paintings, sculpture and other evidence of the Winchester School of the second half of the twelfth century give clear indications of the wealth of a patron such as Henry of Blois. These creations illustrate a range of materials from the workshops of medieval religious artists in the city. The work of the Winchester School is by any standards outstanding and reveals the world of high art at the end of the period of Winchester's pre-eminence as a royal and ecclesiastical centre. There were many stately bishops after Henry of Blois, but perhaps not even Peter des Roches (died 1238) or Henry Beaufort (died 1447) had the means that Henry of Blois could call upon from his estates, not only as Bishop of Winchester and Abbot of Glastonbury, but also as brother of King Stephen. A great age passed with the death of Bishop Henry in 1171.

Henry II: stability and investment

The accession of Henry II in 1154 brought stability. In 1155 there is evidence in the newly instituted exchequer roll that works were in progress at the castle (**37**). They were standard entries suggesting that works at Winchester were already a regular feature of Stephen's reign. The exceptional characteristic of the exchequer accounts for Winchester Castle is that here alone of all the castles on the royal roll did expenditure on houses and chapels within the castle precinct

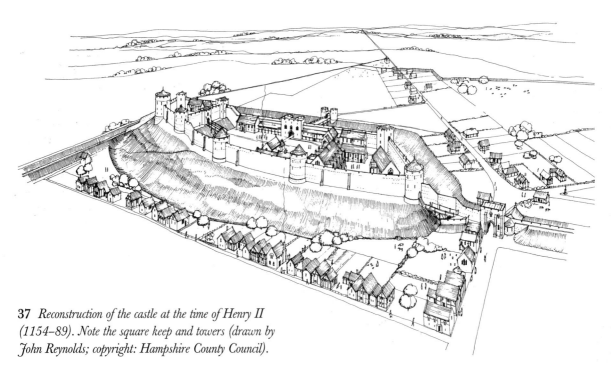

37 *Reconstruction of the castle at the time of Henry II (1154–89). Note the square keep and towers (drawn by John Reynolds; copyright: Hampshire County Council).*

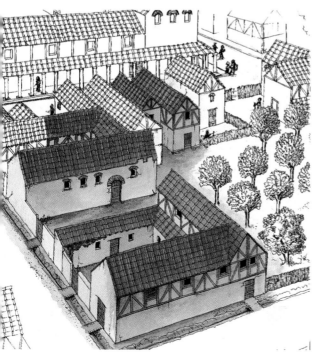

1 *Aerial view of Winchester from the south showing St Catharine's Hill (right), before the M3 extension, and the historic city. Oram's Arbour lies to the left of the cathedral (left) (copyright: Winchester Research Unit).*

2 *Roman Winchester c. AD 300 was spacious. Coloured structures are reconstructed from archaeology at The Brooks (foreground) and Woolworths' site, High Street (centre). The forum buildings (top) run west and south of the site of The Pentice, which covers the whole width of the Roman High Street (after Winchester City Archaeology Office; drawn by Philip Marter).*

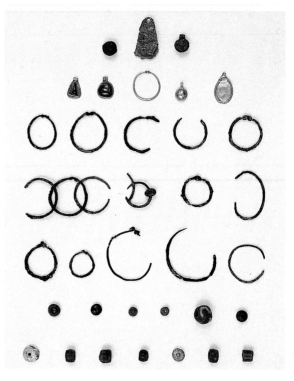

3 *A Saxon necklace of gold, silver, garnets and beads found on the skeleton of an aristocratic and perhaps royal young woman in grave 23, Lower Brook Street c. 650–700. (p.40). The letters on the plan correspond to the catalogue entries in Winchester Studies 7(ii): A–Z (1957–1982), AA–AV (1983–2004). In the colour plate Row 1 (1961, 1957, 1962); Row 2 (1958–9, 1989, 1963, 1960); Row 3 1965, 1969–72; Row 4 (1974–5, 1991 with 1978, 1980–2); Row 5 (1983, 1985–7, 1990); Row 6 (1992–7); Row 7 (1998–2004) (copyright: Winchester Research Unit).*

4 *Norman crypt of the cathedral: east end of the central chamber looking north. The crypt is the earliest work in the cathedral and preserves the plan of the Norman apse, now lost above-ground. The well lies approximately at the geometrical centre of the apse and the original high altar was placed, purposefully, directly above it (photograph and copyright: John Crook).*

5 *Reconstruction of the Old Bishop's Palace at Wolvesey, looking north-east. The bishop's chapel in the foreground, rebuilt in the later Middle Ages, is still in use (drawn by Terry Ball; copyright: English Heritage, 1986).*

6 *An illuminated capital from the Winchester Bible, associated with Henry of Blois, c. 1160. A bishop, perhaps Henry himself, holds a book (copyright: Dean and Chapter).*

7 *St John, the prophet Zephaniah and St James, part of Thomas of Oxford's glazing scheme of the 1390s for Winchester College chapel. These panels are now in the Victoria and Albert Museum (copyright: Royal Commission on Historic Monuments (England) (RCHME)).*

8 *1417. Plans of institutions' lands. The Church dominates the suburbs; within the walls St John's Hospital and the city are dominant (drawn by Judith Dobie after Winchester Research Unit; copyright: English Heritage).*

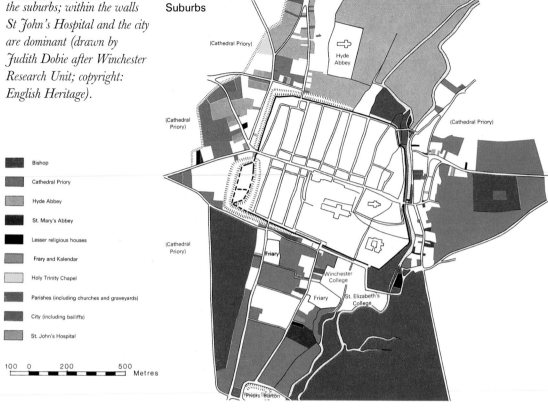

Suburbs

(Hyde Abbey)
(Cathedral Priory)
Hyde Abbey
(Cathedral Priory)
(Cathedral Priory)
(Cathedral Priory)
(Cathedral Priory)
Friary
Winchester College
Friary
St. Elizabeth's College
Priors Barton

Bishop
Cathedral Priory
Hyde Abbey
St. Mary's Abbey
Lesser religious houses
Frary and Kalendar
Holy Trinity Chapel
Parishes (including churches and graveyards)
City (including bailiffs)
St. John's Hospital

100   0   200   500
Metres

9 *1590. Plans of institutions' lands. The lands of the bishop and of the dean and chapter (successors of the cathedral priory) survive unimpaired. Within the walls the city government have benefited since the Reformation (drawn by Judith Dobie after Winchester Research Unit; copyright: English Heritage).*

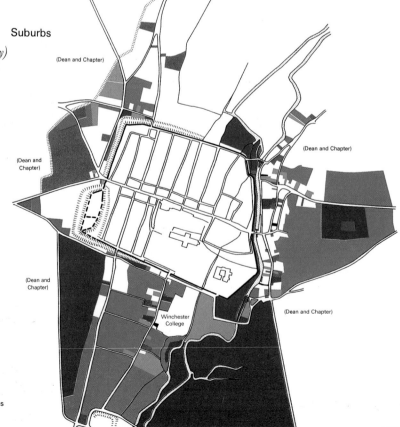

Suburbs

(Dean and Chapter)
(Dean and Chapter)
(Dean and Chapter)
(Dean and Chapter)
(Dean and Chapter)
(Dean and Chapter)
Winchester College

Bishop
Dean and Chapter
Hospitals and colleges
City
Parishes (including churches and graveyards)
St. John's Hospital
Winchester College

100   0   200
Metres

Friary

Friary

St. Mary's Abbey

Cathedral Priory

Wolvesey Palace

100   0   200   500
|___|___|▬▬▬|▬▬▬|▬▬▬|
                    Metres

Cathedral Close

Wolvesey Palace

100   0   200
|___|___|▬▬▬▬▬|
                Metres

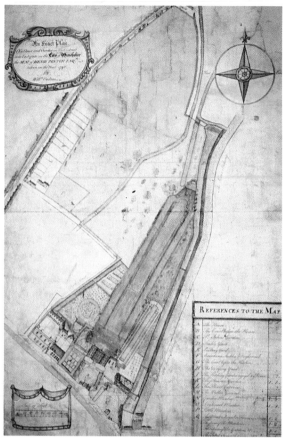

10 *1748. St John's House (left) and chapel. Henry Penton's mansion and garden (centre) are on the former Blackfriars site near East Gate (copyright: Hampshire Record Office, 147M86W/1).*

11 *1801. Cathedral choir. The altar soundboard (1635) and organ-case figures (c. 1665) are preserved in the Triforium; the screen-urns are lost (photograph: John Crook; copyright: Dean and Chapter).*

12 *1993. Twyford Down during the removal of over two million cubic metres of chalk for motorway construction. As 'extreme and irreversible an act of environmental spoiling as can be imagined' thundered* The Times *leader. (copyright: Twyford Down Association).*

exceed expenditure on defence in the period to 1189. So, either the castle defences were in good condition or, because he lacked the facilities at the palace site which had been put to other uses, the king needed the castle to double as a palace. There is nothing to suggest further palace works near the cathedral.

Henry ruled from the borders of Scotland to the Pyrenees. It was from Anjou that his dynasty took its name, there its heartlands lay, and there at the convent of Fontevrault that he was buried. Royal Winchester was less significant than at any time since the Norman Conquest. Moreover, the Angevin connection tended to favour the development of Southampton.

Henry, an enthusiastic hunter and hawker, conducted business as he travelled. At Winchester he built a birdhouse at the castle in the 1170s and established his 'Hawkheye' outside the walls to the north-west of the city, near the site of the new Hampshire Record Office. Royal huntsmen, hawks and hounds occupied this complex where timber and stone structures were revealed in excavations in 1985 (see **75**).

On several occasions Henry found himself embroiled in wars against his wife Eleanor and his sons. Perhaps in response to the rebellion of his son 'young Henry', the king carried out defensive works at Winchester Castle in 1173–4. Here Queen Eleanor was imprisoned after her children rebelled. Henry's relations with his family were the subject of an allegorical mural painting in Winchester Castle, depicting an eagle on its nest being attacked by its young. Work in the castle precinct in the 1170s evidenced another failure in Henry II's life: the murder of Archbishop Becket. A chapel dedicated to Becket was created, with another dedicated to the Breton St Judoc whose relics were at Hyde Abbey. A treasury, a gaol and a herb garden were also built.

Richard I and John

When Henry II died in 1189 Winchester had already entered a period of eclipse as a capital. Richard (1189–99) had spent most of his life abroad and continued to do so. However, he came to Winchester for a coronation in 1189 and returned in 1194 for a second coronation, staying at the castle, from where he made his way to the cathedral. His mother Eleanor watched the coronation from high in the south transept.

National administration, well established by Henry II, continued effectively during Richard's absences. During the Lionheart's reign Winchester Castle enjoyed fifth place in expenditure behind the Tower, Dover, Oxford and York. Richard died in 1199, after which the throne passed to his brother John (1199–1216), among the most mobile of English kings. In his seventeen-and-a-half-year reign he never spent more than a month in one place. Thus it is not surprising to find Winchester one staging-post among many, and in the course of his reign it fell to eighteenth in terms of residential expenditure.

During Richard and John's reigns the city developed its privileges. Unlike episcopal towns where the domination of the bishop could be absolute, Winchester enjoyed divided lordship after Henry II took back the royal properties which were in Henry of Blois's hands in 1148. In honour of his coronation at Winchester in 1189 (and no doubt with an associated financial settlement by the city), Richard confirmed the privileges of the city's gild merchant (see Glossary), and gave added permission for it to plead cases outside the walls, a freedom of urban life sought after in the Middle Ages. City walls were another proof of urban identity. Winchester had developed its own seal by *c.* 1200 which shows five crenellated gate towers. As in many towns, the gild merchant became synonymous with the city government *c.* 1200 and the first reference to a mayor is found around this date (**38**).

John's reign was a watershed in terms of grants of city charters. In 1215, the same year as Magna Carta, he granted a charter (no longer extant) to Winchester confirming its privileges. After Runnymede, in the civil war between king and barons, the latter supported by Louis, son of Philip II of France, Winchester Castle was captured after two weeks' siege. The attacking baronial army under Louis filled the ditch and

38 *The city's thirteenth-century moot horn, now displayed in the City Museum. It was sounded to summon the freemen's assembly. Measurements (max. diameter) 58.5 by 9.9cm (23 by 4in); weight 6kg (13lb), cast in bronze. It is decorated with bishops and lions – perhaps representing Church and State, the joint masters of the city (photograph: John Crook).*

39 *Reconstruction of the castle in the time of Henry III (1216–72). Parts of the round towers are displayed north of the Great Hall (see **40**) (drawn by John Reynolds; copyright: Hampshire County Council).*

breached the walls. However, with John's death the point of the war was lost and in 1217 the castle, after having been battered by attacks from both within and without the walls of the city, was recaptured for Henry III.

Henry III and Peter des Roches

Henry III (1216–72) was the most enthusiastic monarch for Winchester. He was born there in 1207, baptized in the cathedral, and during his minority came under the influence of its bishop, Peter des Roches (1205–38). This great bishop

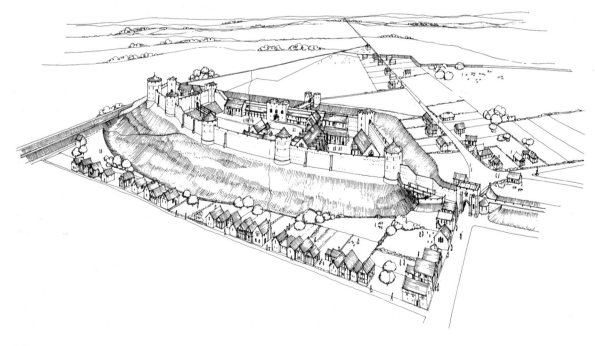

was an engineer and diplomat as well as one of the few crusaders to enter Jerusalem at the head of an army (in 1229). The king's obvious love of fine architecture, which he did much to improve in the city, may have been derived from des Roches. Henry spent Christmas at Winchester eighteen times in his fifty-six-year reign.

Building work at Winchester is often loosely described as Henry III's. Early in the reign, however, Peter des Roches was the moving force. His campaign involved major works, notably the replacement after 1222 of the square keep of the castle by a functional, fashionable round one. This was followed by remodelling of the towers of the castle in the new rounded style (**39**). In the same year he began the rebuilding of the castle Great Hall at a cost of £500. This magnificent building is the finest example of secular work from Henry III's reign still in existence (**40**), although later altered in building campaigns of the fourteenth and nineteenth centuries. Henry III spent £10,000 in Winchester during his reign, when chapels as well as chambers, decorated in green and embellished with stars, were added to the castle.

Archaeological excavation and detailed study of mortars have shown that the city walls were rebuilt in the thirteenth century. This rebuilding may have accompanied the campaigns in the last year of John's reign or, alternatively, was a reaction to the failure of the walls to keep out John's opponents. If the latter, then Bishop des Roches may well have been the architect. The thirteenth-century rebuilding of the Roman wall was substantial, involving a refacing with ashlar blocks and flints. The largest section of the city walls still to be seen is found south of Wolvesey and along The Weirs, standing to a height of some 6m (20ft).

If work on the castle and city walls was a benefit of the minority period, so was the granting of a charter to the city in 1227. It echoed the Johannine charter of 1215, but with additional clauses, perhaps the most important of which was the promise that the royal mint would remain in Winchester for ever. However, the young king could not sustain that promise, and sixteen years later in 1243, the final coins were struck at the Winchester mint. Moneyers had long been significant members of society in Winchester, and their disappearance represents a diminution of royal patronage.

As one benefit ceased, another began. Two mills in the Coitebury area (around Eastgate Street), granted to the city by Henry III, were perhaps in themselves useful but not outstanding gifts. However, from these small property holdings – the first to be owned by the city government – grew wealth which made the city authorities rivals to the king and the Church as landlords within its walls. Ultimately the corporation was to outstrip other landowners, gaining some 30 per cent of property in the city after the Reformation (see **colour plates 8** and **9**).

On his return from the Holy Land in 1231 Bishop des Roches set in place a new jurisdiction in the southern and eastern suburbs of the city, perhaps to secure income from these areas. These extra-mural lands were known collectively as The Soke, and were extended by Bishop William Raleigh (1240–50) to include part of the street outside West Gate and a similar area outside North Gate. These represent substantial areas and reflect not only the power and organizational ability of Bishop Peter, but also growth in population.

The Barons' War

Poor relations between Henry III (who prevented the bishop gaining access to his diocesan lands until 1244) and Bishop Raleigh were indicative of increasingly bad relations with the nobility and churchmen which culminated in the Barons' War of 1263–7. Henry III carried out considerable work on the castle: in 1243 the ditch was widened; in the 1250s work continued on the defences so that by 1258, when violence flared, all the towers in its eastern wall (against the city) had been rebuilt, rounded and high to the best contemporary specifications.

Raleigh's successor was the king's young half-brother Aymer of Lusignan (otherwise known as

40a *(opposite:) Winchester Castle Great Hall, built under Bishop des Roches, overseen by Elias de Dereham, c. 1222–36 (photograph: John Crook).*

40b *Winchester Castle Great Hall. The elevation and section show how the hall might have looked in its thirteenth-century form. Traces of the upstanding window openings can be seen above the fourteenth-century windows (right) in* **40a** *(drawn by Philip Marter).*

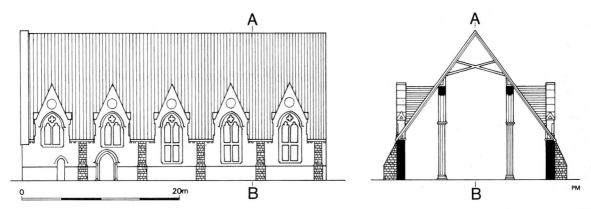

de Valence; 1250–60) who contributed a Purbeck screen to enclose the shrine of St Swithun (**41**). However, he paid a price for being a foreigner and for his relationship with the king, as the focus of the conflict in the summer of 1258 was a siege by baronial forces of his Wolvesey Palace, and he was expelled from England.

Perhaps also in 1258–9, possibly because the economy of the city was ailing and so interruptions to trade the more unfortunate, further tensions became apparent between groups in the city. City people alleged that the prior and monks

had blocked various city gates by which traders came to market. Such measures may have been part of a defensive scheme against the baronial besiegers of Wolvesey. The baronial forces enjoyed sufficient success in 1258 to force the king to agree to the Provisions of Oxford. But the tide turned for Henry III and in 1261 a parliament at the castle hall at Winchester repudiated the Provisions.

41 *A reconstruction of fragments, now on display in the Triforium Gallery, of a Purbeck shrine, probably Swithun's (drawing and copyright: John Crook).*

Some, perhaps limited, royalist support in the city, together with the strengthened defences of the castle, enabled the king on this occasion to reward the city with this symbolic ceremony.

However, the king's temporary victory did not eradicate tensions between sectors of the population of Winchester. In 1264, a week before Henry III was captured at the battle of Lewes, Winchester citizens attacked the cathedral priory burning both the King's and Prior's Gates. The king took hasty action to protect the Winchester Jews who were under attack in the confused political circumstances of the time. In the final flush of baronial success before their cause was destroyed and Simon de Montfort killed at the battle of Evesham in August 1265, Winchester was captured by the younger Simon de Montfort, an event accompanied by further attacks on Jews in the city. The castle held out, although there was damage to property in its vicinity during the fighting.

After 1265 Henry III enjoyed seven years of personal rule. His death in 1272 represents the end of an era in the city. He was the first post-Conquest monarch to be buried at Westminster Abbey. This was the opening move in the creation of a mausoleum in England to match that of the Capetian dynasty at St Denis, outside Paris. Winchester Castle remained a strongpoint, but building there all but ceased after 1272.

The Jewish community

By the middle of the thirteenth century, Jews had become a powerful force in the city. That de Montfort was against them and Henry III for them can be confidently asserted: no doubt because by borrowing from the Jews Henry could side-step the need for parliamentary grants. With the return of Henry III's personal rule after 1265, the Jews prospered in Winchester, based around Jewry Street.

In 1268 Benedict the Jew was admitted freeman of the gild merchant, the earliest surviving record of any admission to the guild, and no doubt an event worthy of record. But de Montfort was not the only enemy of the Jews, as is evidenced by the need to issue a further edict for their protection in 1270, in which year the cathedral priory agreed to pay the large sum of £100 as damages to Winchester Jewry. Nationally the Jewish community was already unpopular with Edward I, Henry III's son and successor, when in 1287 Assher the Jew etched his name in the wall of the castle while imprisoned there. Finally, in 1290, all Jews were expelled from England.

Edward I

Edward I (1272–1307) did not return from crusading until 1274. The king, well known for his Welsh castles, saw that Winchester Castle was maintained and that works were done, such as the rebuilding of the bridge over the ditch at the western entrance. Winchester's association with King Arthur may have been the reason why, in the wake of the rediscovery of 'Arthur's grave' at Glastonbury, a round table was made. The Arthurian connection cannot be proved, but the table, still to be seen hanging on the wall of the Great Hall, was made c. 1290 (**42**). So far as Edward I was concerned, the myth of Arthur was propaganda against the Welsh, but became entwined with the folklore of Winchester.

Winchester served Edward I in a number of ways. It provided a solemn setting for the enactment of the Statute of Winchester (1285) which concerned the keeping of the peace. On other occasions it was a secure prison for a range of offenders, including Jews and, after 1290, Welsh and then Scots military prisoners.

Although Winchester was not a favourite haunt of Edward's first wife, Eleanor of Castile, a tile representation of her coat of arms has been recovered in the city. A plausible reconstruction of an Eleanor of Castile garden has been created on the south side of the Great Hall of the castle in recent years. The garden has turf seats, an open water-channel with a fountain (modelled on one mentioned in the records at the king's hawkhouse at Charing Cross), an arbour with a camomile lawn and a pleached

42 *The Round Table in 1873. It was clearly once a table as can be seen by the broken mortices which formerly contained the legs (copyright: Hampshire Record Office 65M89/2250 (part)).*

alley. Plants are restricted to those known to have been favoured in the thirteenth century.

The friars

The contrast between the wealth of kings and bishops of Winchester and their ancient priory and the poverty of the orders of friars, which arrived in England in the 1220s, is as sharp as any distinction to be made in the Middle Ages. The friars came to England fired with zeal to live in poverty and help the urban poor in particular. At Winchester the Dominicans gained an extensive site to establish a major house, inside East Gate to the north of the High Street: the availability of land within the walls may be an early indication of shrinkage of population and settlement, for at Oxford and elsewhere they had to be content with extra-mural sites. As was so common for religious communities whose mission was to serve the poor, the Franciscans and Dominicans found themselves the receivers of donations, and in time their friaries became popular as desirable burial places. Their houses at Winchester, as elsewhere, became comparatively richly appointed as the recovery of high-status glazed tiles from their East Gate site shows.

One nuance of social and religious change which can be demonstrated by archaeology from the thirteenth century was the emergence of the practice of burial within the nuns' church at St Mary. With the arrival of the friars, whose house became a popular burial place for the wealthy no doubt in return for generous funds for the poor, it could be argued that the nuns needed to have something special to offer their patrons: looking after the remains of patrons and ancestors by nuns at Fontevrault is well attested.

People and buildings

If the city population fell to some 8000 just before 1150 it may have benefited from the marked population rise in the country at large in the century that followed. In 1300 the population may have been stagnating at 8000 but more likely had grown to about 11,625, including the suburbs.

The city was dominated by the great monuments of king and Church. The built environment of their contemporary townspeople has usually to be recovered by excavation. There are no complete standing houses of the period 1150–1300, although in Chesil Street in The Soke most of the original roof of a timber-framed house of the late thirteenth century has recently been discovered intact and has been dated by dendrochronology to the winter of 1292–3: a unique survival of that period and the oldest dated town house in Hampshire.

Excavation has revealed much about living conditions among dwellers in the city in the twelfth and thirteenth centuries. Excavations at Lower Brook Street (1960s) and The Brooks (1987–8) have revealed evidence of housing of this date. At present such information as there is on these structures is available only from interim reports, supported by the finds volumes from the 1960s' excavations.

A two-storeyed, flint rubble house set back from the street, for example, was already in place in Lower Brook Street by 1150. Its narrow, splayed windows, of a kind often found in churches, are typical of the period. The space between this house and the street was occupied by flimsy wooden structures, no doubt shops and/or workshops. It is clear that there was a mixture of high-status stone and timber-framed houses built together in this area of the city. One timber building, known as Lower Brook Street, House I, was a simple, single-storeyed timber structure which developed into a complex stone structure of two storeys combining domestic and industrial premises by 1200 (see **45**).

Just to the north, The Brooks excavations revealed a similar pattern of both stone and timber houses and workshops. On the Upper Brook Street (de Tytynge) site, the single, wooden tenement of tenth- or eleventh-century date was divided into

43 *Upper Brook Street, looking east. The central property, with gates to the street and a hall and other buildings behind, had a complex development from before the Norman Conquest, perhaps being at its most substantial c. 1300 when it belonged to John de Tytynge, alderman of the street. The fuller's property (top left) faced Middle Brook Street (after Graham Scobie, drawn by Philip Marter).*

three tenements in the twelfth century, the buildings being reconstructed in stone. On the Middle Brook Street side of the site a fuller's property of twelfth-century date apparently stood on the street frontage with wooden structures and workshops behind. In both cases the street frontages had been covered by subsequent street widening (itself an indication of the dereliction of this area in the post-medieval period), which left the archaeologists struggling to re-create the fronts of the houses, although arrangements towards the rear of the sites were more easy to recover and interpret (**43**).

Limit of view →
shown below

PLAN

What is plain from present evidence is that in the Brooks area there was mixed housing in the twelfth and thirteenth centuries, and industrial zoning, with ample evidence of activities involved with the textile industry to the fore. Analysis from the 1960s' excavations shows a clear rise in quantity of finds of thirteenth-century date, which is consistent with high population and the prosperity characterized by the major monuments.

Churches

The twelfth and thirteenth centuries saw a peak in the number of churches in Winchester, both within and outside the walls. The total, about 1300, was made up of the cathedral priory, 2 abbeys, 4 friaries, 4 non-parochial chapels (not including various private chapels, for example at the castle) and 54 parish churches. The distribution of the parish churches which have been located can be seen on the 1148 map (see **36**), with a concentration around the wealthy High Street. Of this great body of churches only 7 are now standing, and these have limited twelfth- and thirteenth-century work. Excavation has taken

place on 7 demolished churches, most notably St Mary, Tanner Street, and St Pancras, both adjacent in the Brooks area. These show development and expansion in the twelfth and thirteenth centuries. At St Peter in Macellis, St George Street, there were enlargements which included the addition of an apse of some 3m (10ft) in diameter, and a north aisle probably built in the twelfth or thirteenth century. In similar fashion at St Anastasius, the siting of the north wall further north in the late thirteenth century suggests the incorporation of an aisle. At the surviving St John in The Soke a fine series of thirteenth-century wall paintings was still to be seen in the nineteenth century, when they were largely destroyed, although subsequent clearance of blocked thirteenth-century windows revealed surviving fragments of that scheme in the splays where representations of St John the Evangelist and St Christopher are found. As a whole the evidence from the parish churches is consistent with the recorded growth of the city and with well-attested trends in church architecture in the two centuries before 1300.

6

War and plague

1300–1485

The city was as populous in 1300 as at any time in the Middle Ages, but the following two centuries saw significant decline. Developments in the built environment are more readily comprehensible to the modern eye, for many types of structures created at this time still remain. With the notable exception of the building on the west side of Chesil Street mentioned above, this is the first period for which domestic properties survive in the city both within the walls and in the suburbs.

The cathedral took on the form in which we see it today, with the demolition of the Norman western towers and their replacement after 1350 with a great window in Perpendicular style. In The Close, the remains of the monastic buildings which survive today include notable timber-framed structures of the fourteenth and fifteenth centuries. The church of St Cross was completed after 1350, and its residential accommodation replaced by 1450. Winchester College appeared in the southern suburb by 1400, an indication of the availability of land after the Black Death. The West Gate as we see it today is largely late fourteenth century in form.

Many buildings, not in existence in 1150, would have been visible to visitors in the fourteenth and fifteenth centuries, but have since disappeared. The friaries, especially the Dominican and Franciscan houses inside the East Gate, were notable additions in the thirteenth century, and became more substantial as the friars' urban mission was rewarded with donations in the later Middle Ages.

Royal influence wanes in this period, and ecclesiastical developments – for example at the cathedral priory, St Cross, Winchester College and at Wolvesey – mask a general decline in the city's economy, which led to some 'fossilization' which accounts for the comparatively numerous late medieval standing remains surviving today. Parish churches, however, began to decline in numbers, and many disappeared.

The principal features of the fourteenth- and fifteenth-century layout were: the streets, the scale of the domestic and shop accommodation in relation to the great buildings of cathedral and bishop's palace, and market places such as that marked by the Buttercross in the High Street. Many areas of the city, especially north of the High Street and in the suburbs, reverted to gardens, particularly in the fifteenth century. Round the High Street and elsewhere, the form of plots preserves the dimensions of late medieval gardens, and leases of property make reference to such appurtenances.

The end of royal residence

When fire broke out in the royal apartments in the castle in 1302 Edward I and Queen Margaret were asleep but managed to escape. Full repairs were probably never carried out at the castle. This marks a key stage in the reduction of Winchester's royal role. However, occasional high-status finds from the castle – such as a green glass goblet, indicative of wine-drinking, from the period *c.* 1300 – illuminate the quality of life in that late stage of royal use.

From early in the fourteenth century the royal entourage usually stayed at Wolvesey. There was considerable political uncertainty in the 1320s and 1330s: civil war, followed by war with France. The city probably favoured Edward II (1307–27) in the struggle against his queen, Isabella. Winchester was established as a wool staple town in 1326 and retained that status until 1353. The loss of the civil war by Edward II led to retribution. Thus the Earl of Winchester was beheaded by Isabella's supporters in 1327 at Bristol and his head transported to Winchester Castle to be displayed above its gate.

War against France

The end of the Capetian dynasty in 1328 made possible an English claim to the throne of France. This claim led to war with France: the Hundred Years War broke out in 1337. A destructive raid on Southampton in October 1338 caused alarm in Hampshire and works on the Winchester walls were carried out in 1338–9.

The early years of the war were extravagantly financed so that by 1340 the treasury was empty and there was a crisis. The remarkable wool weights which survive in Winchester from this time, no doubt associated with the city's status as a staple town, may have been part of a drive for greater revenue.

War dragged on until 1453 and affected the city intermittently. For example, after 1369 when the French threatened the south coast, royal orders were issued for the repair of the walls and these orders perhaps led to the repointing of the walls of Winchester with yellow mortar and flints which have been found embedded in such mortar in the west, north and east walls of the city. The machicolations and grand refurbishment of the West Gate are also suggestive of a late fourteenth-century date (see **31**). Durn Gate was rapidly walled up at this time at the insistence of a local alderman.

By *c.* 1400 the castle was not always fit for royal visitors. Visits by Richard II and Anne of Bohemia (1393), and by Henry V in 1415, involved ecclesiastical accommodation: in Richard's reign Bishop Wykeham was the host; in Henry V's reign it was Cardinal Beaufort, the king's cousin. However, when Henry IV and Joan of Navarre came to Winchester in 1402 for their marriage they stayed at the castle, perhaps because Bishop Wykeham was too elderly to receive them (p. 84).

In the 1420s during the minority of Henry VI the history of the ancient capital was being carefully managed. About 1425 a mortuary chest, said to contain the remains of kings Egbert and Kenulph, was replaced with a fine painted chest, now to be seen on display in the Triforium Gallery. Not only was the Lancastrian dynasty vulnerable during a minority and so needed bolstering in all possible ways, but also Cardinal Beaufort was illegitimate. His grand coat of arms with the motif of his cardinal's hat, still to be seen displayed in the hall at St Cross, was intended to give substance to a member of a family barred by statute from the throne.

Plague and population

With the loss of royal status and a levelling off of population from the late thirteenth century, growth in the city slackened. The Black Death of 1348–50 ushered in three centuries in which demographic development was dominated by plague. This disease and its economic effects added to the difficulties Winchester was encountering with the loss of royal status. There is some doubt about when and where the plague broke out. The chronicler Knighton claimed Southampton was the port of entry, and it may have been. In October 1348 Bishop Edington of Winchester issued mandates for prayers to be offered because of the plague. By Christmas 1348 the disease had taken a grip. Urban populations were especially at risk from the plague and Winchester was no exception with its dense housing, malnutrition and poor sanitation.

Evidence from the Brooks excavations in the 1960s showed evidence in anaerobic deposits of parasites and plague bacilli. The effects of the plague on the clergy of the city and diocese can be charted in Bishop Edington's register.

Winchester diocese was hit hardest in England with an estimated 48 per cent mortality among clergy. The cathedral priory was hard pressed and numbers fell from around 60 before the plague to some 35 thereafter until the Dissolution. At the 'Sustren Spital', a hospital community of women in the southern suburb, there were normally 21 inmates, but after the plague this fell to 6, increasing to 10 in 1352–3 but never to more than 16 thereafter. Men were admitted in the later Middle Ages. The effects on the lay population of the city are more difficult to monitor, but we do know that a dispute was carried to the royal government about graveyard space around the cathedral where the high death toll filled up the available plots and led to encroachments on adjacent property. In February 1352 a royal grant was made because of the 'waste and depression in the city from the time when the deadly pestilence last prevailed'. Winchester was among places devastated by the Black Death. Plague returned fiercely in 1361 and regularly thereafter.

Population and cemeteries
The tarrage roll for 1417 lists 839 tenements excluding The Soke, which perhaps contained 40 per cent of the population. This information can be translated into 6921 lay people and an estimated 789 clergy – total 7710. These figures represent a decline from the higher estimated population in 1300, but are on a par with the lower estimate. By 1450 the population had more certainly declined when petitions from the city to the central government referred to 997 empty houses in the city. The population probably decreased towards the end of the fifteenth century.

It is possible from their excavated bones to make some comments about the physical and medical characteristics of the inhabitants of the city in the three centuries preceding 1450. Many bones were uncovered in the 1960s and preliminary results show that arthritis afflicted the majority of Winchester skeletons analysed; there were a number of bone tumours – some perhaps tubercular, others carcinogenic. In a small number of instances syphilis or an allied disease may be indicated by a roughening of the bone surface, particularly on the long bones. It is worth noting that plague, among other diseases, leaves no mark upon the bones.

Thirty-six graves, presumably of patrons and their families and of nuns, have been excavated from St Mary's Abbey. These human remains date from the mid-thirteenth century down to the Dissolution. An equal number of men and women were buried in the nunnery. Seven females lived to over forty-five: none of the men did. Whether or not the women came from the abbey is unknown, but dietary deficiency together with arthritis and other diseases can be shown to have affected people even at this exalted level of society.

The Great Revolt
The Great or Peasants' Revolt of 1381 over the poll tax provided an opportunity for a general settling of disputes. Potential existed for friction between ecclesiastical and lay society in Winchester and, echoing the thirteenth century, this may have been one of the motives for violence in the city in 1381. However, it may have been that the immense wealth of the see and the priory took some of the force out of such feelings, for these institutions offered sustained economic activity in the great building campaigns of the later fourteenth and fifteenth centuries.

Anger was directed primarily against the royal government. Fourteen out of twenty-five of those recorded in Hampshire who were executed or who fled after the Revolt came from Winchester. The focus of the Revolt was the lower High Street in the cloth-finishing area of the city: Tanner Street, Colebrook Street and the area around the church of St George. William Wygge, perhaps the ringleader, was involved with others at Winchester and elsewhere. He was a member of the guild with responsibilities in local government: the Revolt was by no means only a peasant affair. Wygge obtained a pardon and went on to be five times mayor of the city.

Housing and industry

The period after the plague of 1348 was difficult for the city. The housing stock varies and there is archaeological and documentary evidence that properties went out of use. However, fine housing of late fourteenth-century date survives in the city, for example The Blue Boar (**44**) in the eastern suburb. However, the wealth and the status of some who took part in the Great Revolt, and the survival of a contemporary house, do not indicate that everyone in Winchester was prosperous at this time. Four single-cell cottages each *c.* 1.6sq m (17sq ft) in area, perhaps the flimsiest houses from the fourteenth century excavated in England, were laid bare in the 1960s adjacent to St Pancras Lane (Lower Brook Street) (**45**). These houses and those adjacent were very dark. The medieval houses excavated at Lower Brook Street produced no fewer than 105 lamps out of 126 excavated in the city in the 1960s. Two houses alone produced over 60 lamps between them, fuelling the interpretation that the activity carried on in these premises required long hours of indoor work. At higher-status properties where there were more windows, more costly wax candles were used: this produced proportionately more candle holders among the finds there and fewer lamps in the archaeological record.

Excavation of a tenement, gable end to the street and facing on to Middle Brook Street, revealed it to be of artisan status and more substantial than the single-cell properties on Lower Brook Street. It was extended in the late fourteenth or early fifteenth century by the addition of a workshop and fuller's tank (which drained into the Middle Brook), identified by traces of ammonia and fuller's earth.

By 1400 clothworking in Winchester was in a state of flux. The withdrawal of the cloth industry from the city to the countryside, and the resultant impoverishment and depopulation of the city, was prominent among the reasons given by the Winchester city government in a petition to the royal government for a reduction in taxation made in 1440 and sent a second time in 1452.

Evidence can readily be adduced to show how the city changed both demographically and economically after the Black Death. From the time of the 1361 plague onwards, the land of Godbegot, for example, was parcelled up and the principal tenement of the 'manor' was broken up and let out. Elsewhere the great tenement of John de Tytynge on Upper Brook Street (see **43**) appears to have suffered a similar fate, being broken up and used by lesser folk.

Interpretation of such evidence, however, is uncertain at present, raising as well as answering questions. Were the wealthy moving elsewhere in the city, and if so, where? Was it to The Soke, east of the city, where houses such as The Blue Boar and the Old Chesil Rectory (which was not built as a rectory) are found? In the High Street, 33 and 34 (in The Pentice) and the Godbegot are all post-plague and before 1500 (**46**). Documentary evidence of the subdivision of tenements suggests crowding together of poorer people, but overall the evidence indicates a general fall in population of the city.

It is unsafe to argue on the basis of surviving vernacular houses and shops alone: their survival represents no more than a fossilization of Winchester after this period. Photographs of

44 *The Blue Boar, 24 and 25 St John Street, in 1942, before extensive renovation. The curved timbers of the north elevation are a key element in dating the structure to the fourteenth century (copyright: RCHME).*

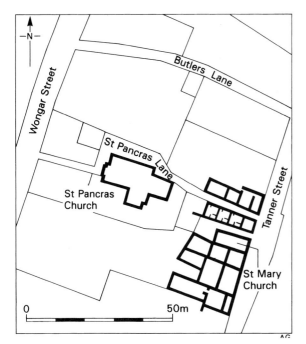

45 *This map is a microcosm of what is known from documentary sources and the results of excavation. The fourteenth-century cottages south of St Pancras Lane were flimsy. The easternmost of these properties was served by a water course at this time, and a hearth in its neighbour to the west hinted at dyeing. The southerly house on this plan, standing back from the street, was a substantial stone structure built before 1150. It was extended to the street frontage as space was at a premium c. 1200. The neighbourhood is shown in its fourteenth-century phase with the churches of St Pancras and St Mary Tanner Street (after Winchester Research Unit: redrawn by Alejandra Gutierrez).*

46 *Reconstruction of 33, 34 and plan of 35 (part) High Street. These shops, recently dated by dendrochronology to 1459, were built at right angles to the street. They comprised purpose-built shops beside The Pentice walk with living accommodation above and behind the shops. A fragment of a Wealden house (part of Boots at 35 High Street), dendro-dated to 1340, stands with its roof-ridge parallel to the street. It may originally have had lean-to shops fronting the street. The Pentice, in part at least, assumed its present appearance in 1459. In 1340 it clearly looked very different (drawn by Judith Dobie, English Heritage).*

nineteenth-century Winchester show timber-framed properties now demolished, for example on the corner of the High Street and St Thomas Street, and also the corner of the High Street and Staple Gardens (**47**), and in Middle Brook Street. Taken together – archaeology, standing remains and documentary evidence including photographs and Speed's map of *c.* 1611 – it can be suggested that apart from the ecclesiastical southern half of the city, there was a zoning of new building in the High Street, Middle Brook Street and the eastern suburb in the period 1350–1500. However, numbers of timber-framed buildings did not survive the fifteenth century, for archaeology has shown elsewhere on the Brooks that houses there were demolished at that time and replaced by gardens. For the fullers who remained, these open spaces provided areas for them to dry their cloth as the excavated remains of their drying frames have shown.

There were fortunes to be made, as the speculative developments and mercantile success of Mark le Fayre, mayor, merchant and property developer in the early fifteenth century shows. Le Fayre, among other activities, developed a novel building type, an inn, at The George before 1420. Thereafter inns became more common. The George, probably originally a large courtyard tenement with gates both to north and south,

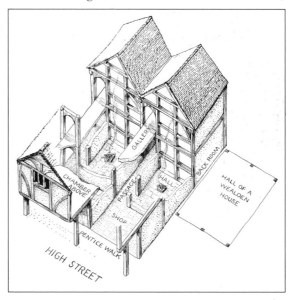

survived for a long period on the north side of the High Street and stood, although much altered, for 500 years until its demolition in 1956.

Features of the city today such as the 13m (43ft) high Buttercross (**48**) in the High Street, which signalled its eponymous market, date from the same period: Cardinal's Beaufort's time. At St Cross fifteenth-century domestic accommodation created for the cardinal's retainers is to be seen, massively built as individual houses, with a communal hall and defensive gate tower. The city markets were serving a new clientele which included Wykeham's collegers.

Le Fayre was a private landlord; the city government extended its land holdings at the same period as an increasingly powerful institutional landlord of Winchester housing and other property. In the exceptional year of 1466–7, rent accounted for 88 per cent of the corporation's income. The city proved as adaptable as ever to changing circumstances.

47 *The Star Inn, 83 High Street, photographed c. 1885 and demolished by 1929, was a medieval jettied structure. The front was bricked over probably in the eighteenth century (copyright: Winchester City Museums, PWCM 3535).*

Living standards

Central government became increasingly concerned in the fourteenth and fifteenth centuries with improving living standards, especially after the Black Death. The Statute of Labourers (1351) was an attempt to force wages back down to pre-plague levels. The Sumptuary Law of 1363 and its successors sought to dictate what people at different levels of society should wear and eat. Anxiety about improved living standards for the lower ranks of society was clearly at fever pitch. The Winchester evidence is anecdotal, but so far as diet is concerned endorses some of the anxieties of the ruling classes.

Winchester evidence for diet in the later Middle Ages hinges on the contents of latrines. The last fill of the latrine of a large house on Upper Brook Street (see **43**) produced a wide variety of evidence of fourteenth-century diet including strawberry, fig, mulberry, cherry and plum, onion and leek as well as a range of herbs and spices – caraway, coriander, dill and parsley. Wholemeal bread consumption is evidenced by wheat and rye bran. Human worms and fleas also found their way into the pit.

The evidence is surprisingly diverse, but in the absence of precise dating material not easy to

interpret. If the contents of the latrine were contemporary with the wealthy merchant John de Tytynge's occupation of the site early in the fourteenth century the materials may suggest some polarizing of the living standards of the population. If they come from later in the century when the structure was abandoned and the site divided, then maybe the last inhabitants of the undivided property took the opportunity in a buyer's market to remove themselves and leave the low-lying site to its fate. It seems unlikely that these remains were the diet of the folk who occupied the declining property. It may simply be that new latrines were dug and an old one abandoned, or that poorer people may have relied more on public conveniences than sustaining their own provision. It may have been that certain secular inhabitants of the city continued to enjoy comfort and plenty perhaps despite declining opportunities for the population as a whole.

One effect of population stagnation and decline was that there was more wealth for those who survived the vicissitudes of the fourteenth century. So religious institutions which had previously found recruitment comparatively easy because of high population and an energetic and respected papacy had to make themselves more appealing in a changing world (pp. 76–7). Thus, evidence from St Mary's Abbey can be seen broadly to match that from the de Tytynge site. Dietary requirements relaxed: in particular meat eating became more common on special occasions and at feasts. Meat bones in late medieval deposits at the nunnery included sheep and pig. A range of both salt-water creatures – sturgeon and dolphin – and freshwater fish from fishponds, was also found. Although this may have been the fare of the abbey guests, the evidence seems clear that some survivors of the famines and plagues of the fourteenth century were able to sustain a good quality of life.

Edington to Wykeham

Bishop Edington had already begun to remodel the cathedral before 1350 when he demolished the westworks, which were not replaced.

48 *The Market Cross, or Buttercross, built in Cardinal Beaufort's time (died 1447). This view, published in 1829, was dedicated to Alexander Baring MP, of The Grange, Northington. It shows the city's medieval fabric and pump, and also the improved paving brought about by the eighteenth-century commissioners. Wooldridge, whose shop is seen on the corner of The Pentice, was a female butcher (drawn by Bartlett; Author's collection).*

Edington's successor was William of Wykeham, a clerk in Edington's household before he was taken into royal service *c.* 1350 as Edward III's clerk of works at Windsor Castle. Wykeham not only gained the diocese but also, like Edington, became Chancellor of England. Wykeham's career draws diverse elements of Winchester's development together in the most positive of ways. So far as the defences were concerned, he had the wall surrounding Wolvesey rebuilt at his own expense which drew on his experience of defensive works at Windsor.

Wykeham's second contribution to the city was Winchester College (**49**). This was conceived

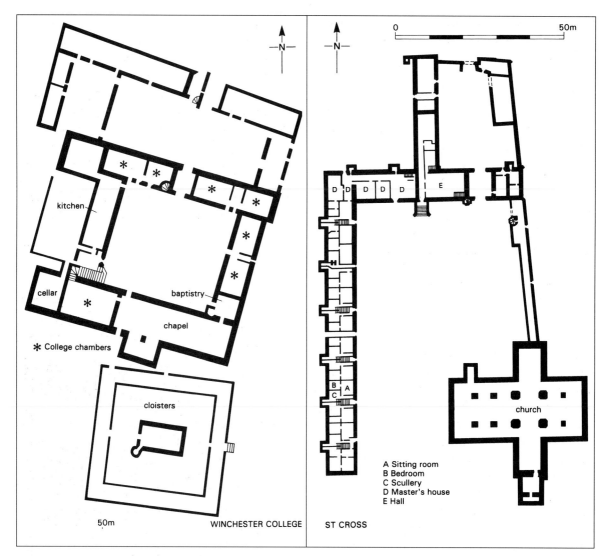

49 *Winchester College (school) by William of Wykeham (died 1404) and St Cross Hospital (accommodation for retired retainers) by Cardinal Beaufort (died 1447): communal buildings of the late fourteenth and early fifteenth centuries, redrawn for comparison to the same scale (after Pevsner et al. (1967) and Winchester College Archaeological Society (1926); redrawn by Alejandra Gutierrez).*

in the 1380s and work was under way by the end of the decade. The intention, as the founder's statutes show, was to produce properly educated clergy to replace those lost in the plague. The college reflects the changing face of the city. It occupies land previously inhabited, but available

in the southern suburb after the Black Death. In addition, French threats no doubt drove suburban dwellers into town. The severe fortified gatehouses of the college bear testimony to the unsettled times in which they were built. The muniment tower is no less strong, and was originally reached only through iron-bound internal doors, one of which is beside the chapel altar. These were secured by large keys, while the documentary evidence of the college's endowments is kept in multi-locked trunks. Wykeham left no doubt as to the supreme importance of the endowments he provided for his college's future. The college buildings are exceptionally fine work of their period and should be visited, especially

Wykeham's hall-over-schoolroom and the chapel built end-on in series with the hall – a match for his similar creations at New College, Oxford and at Windsor.

Wykeham's works at Winchester highlight the balance of power in the city in the later Middle Ages. Apart from his work on the walls and at the college, he continued the enormous task, begun by Edington, of remodelling the nave of the cathedral from Romanesque to the Gothic masterpiece we see today. But remodelling rather than rebuilding is significant. A patron with the unrivalled resources enjoyed by Wykeham did not demolish, as Edington had done before the plague, but rebuilt to good effect. Such is the contrast between high and late medieval architectural works (**50**).

Wykeham emerges as an individual in Renaissance mould – for his building works coincided with Chaucer's *Canterbury Tales*, with their emphasis on the individual pilgrims. Wykeham's individualism is best seen in his chantry chapel, which is an architectural gem, although chantry chapels have been criticized as the privatization of public space. The chantry is in the nave of the cathedral, as if making his mark on the part of the building he had largely remodelled. His lifelike effigy is accompanied by diminutive figures at his feet. The sculpture which adorned the niches of the chantry has disappeared from its original setting, although the scale of certain pieces now in the Triforium Gallery suggests that these fragments originated in his chantry. The very existence of the chantry chapel betokens concerns about death in the post-plague era. Henry Chichele, a boy at Winchester College, who became Archbishop of Canterbury in the early fifteenth century and who like Wykeham founded a school and an Oxford college, was buried in Canterbury Cathedral. There, Chichele's chapel contains a tomb representing the archbishop in full regalia while below is found a grisly cadaver-sculpture, the whole bordered by a gloomy text.

As well as undertaking major works at the college and the cathedral (not to mention his work

at East Meon and elsewhere), Wykeham built extensively at Wolvesey. The fine glazing which we know from documentary sources he added to his works in the palace, must once have matched that at Winchester College (**colour plate 7**) and at New College, Oxford, but, despite the recovery of a good deal of glass from the palace site, nothing significant from Wykeham's campaign was found. Surviving documentation of daily life and occasional feasts at Wolvesey is as vivid as standing remains associated with Wykeham. During the Winchester parliament of 1393 a feast

50 *Drawing by Professor Willis (see* **5a***) demonstrating how the cathedral nave was adapted from Romanesque to Gothic before 1400 (photograph: John Crook).*

for 210 guests with Richard II and Anne of Bohemia cost £10 1s 2d and another on the following day for 367 guests cost £39 15s 3d, compared with a normal daily expenditure on the bishop's household of two or three pounds.

Bishop Wykeham lived to welcome the first Lancastrian king to Winchester in 1402. When Henry IV came to the city to be married to Joan of Navarre the couple enjoyed a magnificent feast at Wolvesey. The Lancastrian kings had respect for Winchester as their uncertain usurping predecessors, the Normans, had done. The resurgence of enthusiasm for the French wars under Henry V saw Wolvesey as the venue for Henry V's entertainment of the French ambassadors in the period preceding the Agincourt campaign in 1415 – reputedly the occasion of the famous 'tennis balls' jibe against the young king. The ambassadors stayed at the Franciscan friary.

Church and city

The Church still dominated Winchester, despite the central weakness of the papacy in the fourteenth and fifteenth centuries (**colour plate 8**). Indeed, it may have been that weakness which enabled government officials such as Edington and Wykeham to secure sees with royal support and to occupy them as grandee bishops. Compared with the economic problems of the laymen in the city, there is plenty of evidence that the Church, so far as the episcopate and the monastic landlords were concerned, flourished in the century after the Black Death, for Cardinal Beaufort continued where Wykeham had left off with works at the cathedral, the virtual refoundation of St Cross and the embellishment of Wolvesey. The three bishops of Winchester in the century after the Black Death died in their beds unlike, for example, Archbishop Sudbury of Canterbury who lost his head in 1381. Edington, Wykeham and Beaufort made their contributions to the city, although they all had weightier responsibilities of state.

Their successor, Bishop Waynflete (1447–86), successfully steered a course through the stormy waters of the Wars of the Roses which followed the loss of the Hundred Years War in 1453. From this period a most remarkable ecclesiastical work of art from the city survives: Bishop Waynflete's great screen, which was completed after 1475. Some of the originally painted sculpture is of outstanding quality (**51**) and was probably undertaken by craftsmen from the Netherlands. The creation of the Triforium Gallery in recent years has enabled the display of the impressive surviving fragments of this great work of art, which was cast down at the Reformation barely half a century after its completion. Corresponding to the beginning of work on this new screen was a rebuilding of Swithun's shrine which led to a great procession in which the relics of the saint were borne through the streets of the city in 1476, before being laid in the new shrine.

Parish churches

The bishops and the monasteries operated in late medieval Winchester from a wealthy, if reduced, base. The economy of the city otherwise was more at risk from the vagaries of demographic and economic change and this, together with changing patterns of alms-giving, affected the parish churches. However, the nineteen closures, 30 per cent of the total, of parish churches in the city from 1350 to 1400 and the seventeen parish churches without incumbents in 1440 tell a different story from the great building works on the bishops' and priors' side.

The handful of the parish churches which survive reveal plenty of evidence in the Decorated and Perpendicular styles of the fourteenth and fifteenth centuries: the fifteenth-century tower of St Lawrence has the same features as that of St John, probably of the same date; various Perpendicular windows at St John, St Peter Chesil and at St Matthew, Weeke in the northern suburb all show a continuing availability of funds for work on parish churches after the Black Death. Support for the older institutions such as the Benedictine monasteries waned with the Middle Ages, but at Winchester the monasteries were wealthy enough to survive, financed by their assets. Refocusing of endowment on the parish churches comes through clearly in the Winchester evidence. Winchester citizens embellished their parish churches according to their means.

What has been revealed by archaeology and study of surviving documentation is clear enough. The cathedral priory and the bishop were stratospherically wealthy, but even they had to tailor their projects according to their substantial though reduced incomes. Works such as on the nave or 'public' area of the cathedral were adaptations rather than rebuildings. Diocesan works and private projects such as Winchester College and St Cross, and the rebuilding of Wolvesey, were achievable within scaled-down budgets. In the secular areas of city there was certainly building, but as yet the study of archaeology and of standing remains has not shown whether the timber-framed structures which survive above-ground were more or less grand than those from the preceding period which have been lost. With its mighty cathedral, bishopric and well-endowed religious houses, and with a renewed spirit among its parishioners and among the merchants and the city government, Winchester was not entirely in the doldrums in the last century of Plantagenet England.

51 *Fragment of the head of a bishop from the cathedral great screen probably complete by 1476 and the sculptures in place soon afterwards (photograph: John Crook; copyright: Dean and Chapter).*

7

Renaissance Winchester

1485–1660

The city changed appearance in the sixteenth and seventeenth centuries, and we have a better idea of developments from contemporary comments (pp. 13ff). The Reformation wrought the most significant change. Nunnaminster and Hyde Abbey were effectively demolished after 1539, as were the conventual buildings of the cathedral priory. The friaries disappeared, and the parish churches which had declined in numbers to some 26 in 1500 were to decline still further to 12 by 1600 through closure and amalgamation.

Tudor and Stuart mansions rose from the rubble of the monasteries and elsewhere in Winchester, especially in the suburbs, as land was more freely available in the wake of the Reformation. At Hyde, in the northern suburb, a residence appeared on the site of the Benedictine house, while the Mason family created a mansion out of the Blackfriars within East Gate. Both these mansions have been demolished. Surviving large houses from this period include The Soke, in Chesil Street in the eastern suburb (see 3), and Moberley's (1571), in Kingsgate Street, south of the city walls.

The great medieval buildings suffered, especially in the Civil War, when there was severe damage to the castle; additional destruction at the cathedral to that caused at the Reformation; and the virtual demolition of the bishop's palace at Wolvesey. The archaeological evidence for the destruction at Wolvesey shows how the windows, for example, were collected together in the northern range and broken up systematically, leaving concentrations of decorated glass and melted lead.

National politics and local administration under the Tudors

The battle of Bosworth in 1485 was remote from Winchester but still affected the city. In 1486 Henry VII's first son was christened in the cathedral. The name Arthur and location for the christening were further steps in the institutionalization of the supposed ancient history of the city. The combination of King Arthur and Winchester's antiquity were grist to the mill of the fledgling dynasty. The baptism was a splendid affair with a procession (albeit only from the prior's lodging, now the Deanery, in The Close), a silver font brought from Canterbury, and the provision of rich cloth and tapestry hangings, some of which survive today in the possession of Winchester College (52). Around this time Henry VII's arms were carved in the cathedral and the remains of Saxon kings, including Kynegils and Aethelwulf, were placed in new chests, one of which survives in the Triforium Gallery. Such commissions boosted the standing of the new dynasty and encouraged people to think of the Tudors as successors to the Saxon kings who had contributed to Winchester's past greatness.

In 1522 the magic of Arthur and Winchester was once more activated, when Henry VIII welcomed Emperor Charles V to the city. In the Great Hall of the castle the Round Table was displayed, newly painted with the Tudor rose and bearing the names of the knights surmounted by a bearded Arthur – surely Henry himself, the first monarch known to have been bearded since Richard II over a century before (53).

52 *Tapestry fragment approximately 2 by 1.5m (6ft 6in by 3ft 3in) showing the union of the roses of Lancaster and York, and traditionally associated with the christening of Prince Arthur at Winchester in 1486. This and other tapestry fragments were apparently saved to Winchester College during the Civil War and two are displayed in Winchester College chapel (Author's collection).*

53 *The Round Table mirrors the union of the roses seen in* **52**. *The table now hangs in the Great Hall. Although made c. 1290 (see* **42**) *it was not painted until Henry VIII's time, c. 1522 (copyright: Hampshire Record Office 56M71/1056).*

Winchester steered an unimpeachable political course during the remainder of the century and into the early Stuart period. The mayor and burgesses were supportive of the Reformation, even taking part in the destruction of Swithun's shrine in 1538. But in 1554 they welcomed the Catholic monarchs Mary and Philip (**54**). In 1559 the city was awarded custody of the castle, and Queen Elizabeth visited on several occasions towards 1600.

A key to this success, particularly under Elizabeth and James I, lay in patrons and MPs. For example, Sir Francis Walsingham, a major figure in Elizabethan politics, was appointed High Steward of Winchester for life in 1582 at St John's House on the Broadway. At around the same time

Thomas Fleming became Recorder and represented the city in the parliaments of the 1580s and 1590s. His fine house, The Soke in Chesil Street, survives and fragments of Renaissance decoration are still found there. Fleming kept abreast of political change at the end of Elizabeth's reign and as Lord Chief Justice presided over the trial of Guy Fawkes following the Gunpowder Plot. He died after a party for his tenants in 1613 (**55**).

Fleming's family and friends were staunch Protestants and assisted the city government in its attempts to contain Catholicism. Over fifty Catholics were listed for the Winchester area in 1581: over 15 per cent of the total for the diocese. Although one priest, John Slade, was executed in the city, the old religion appears usually to have

54 *Bishop Gardiner (died 1555), Bishop of Winchester from 1531. Gardiner's sympathies were with Catholicism. After imprisonment during Edward VI's reign, he was reinstated and officiated at the marriage of Queen Mary and Philip of Spain in 1554. This portrait was recently returned by King Juan Carlos of Spain to hang at Wolvesey. Gardiner's chantry chapel of 1556–8 in the cathedral is striking as a Gothic structure decorated with Renaissance work – as symbolic of changing taste as his episcopate was of changing religion (photograph: Peter Jacobs; by permission of the Lord Bishop of Winchester).*

been treated with disapproval rather than violence. This may have been because there were well-connected recusants such as Lady West, whose house in St Peter Street contained missals, vestments and an altar in 1583, and was one of a number of Catholic households found within the walls and in the suburbs.

Population and social structure

By 1524 Winchester had declined to perhaps a quarter or a third of the size it had been in 1100 – perhaps as few as 2000 or a maximum of 4300 inhabitants. In 1524, 595 households were enumerated. Winchester's population rose to some 5270 around 1550, reflecting a surge in population nationally in the sixteenth century. There was a further rise to approximately 6240 in the early seventeenth century, comparing the evidence of the tarrage rolls of 1417 and 1603. Certainly in neighbouring Southampton the population rose to a peak of 4200 in the 1590s before falling back after 1600. Winchester may have mirrored these developments: the population in like manner falling back in the seventeenth century to perhaps fewer than 5000 during the Civil War. A variety of factors explain these fluctuations: including epidemics of plague, which continued until the 1660s, and the Civil War. In particular the phenomenal growth of London from some 50,000 in 1450 to 575,000 to make it the largest city in Europe by 1700, adversely affected Winchester as it did all towns in central and south-eastern England from Tudor times onwards.

A wealth structure can be deduced from the 1524 lay subsidy – a new tax which caught the population unprepared and so provides a good account of wealth which can be analysed by grouping together those of the same assessment. It has often been argued that in England 30 per cent of the population was too poor to pay. In Winchester over 32 per cent were assessed at £1 – the lowest rate; a further 30 per cent fall into the £2–9 group. This gives a total of over 92 per cent whose goods and wages were valued at under £10. The £10–39 group amounted to over 6 per cent, and those valued at over £40 were just over 1 per cent of the population.

The highest valuation in the city in 1524 was £60 – less than the £100 of several contemporary Southampton merchants. In broad terms the groupings within the tax bands in both towns were very similar. As it was a lay subsidy the clergy do not appear.

The Reformation removed the ecclesiastical props on which the poor had depended for a millennium. The resultant development of the Tudor poor law made the relief of the poor and sick a lay responsibility. Apart from the administration of the poor rate, the city authorities administered funds which came to them through

55 *The tomb of Sir Thomas Fleming, Recorder and MP for Winchester, and his wife Mary James, both natives of Newport, Isle of Wight, at North Stoneham church. Sir Thomas died in 1613 and Mary in 1614 (photograph: John Crook).*

bequests. The outstanding example of this was the foundation in 1607 of Christes Hospital, Symonds Street (**56**), for which the corporation purchased one hundred loads of freestone from the ruins of Hyde Abbey.

56 *Christes Hospital, Symonds Street, established by Peter Symonds in his will of 1586 but not incorporated for twenty years, due to a family dispute. Many stones from Hyde Abbey, which had come into the hands of Symonds's step-father, Richard Bethell, were used in construction of the almshouse, and some are visible here (lower courses and quoins, left) (photograph and copyright: Alex Turner).*

Society in Winchester was turned upside-down during the Civil War in the early 1640s. A despondent former mayor, John Trussell, summed up the effects of billeting in the city:

Now what they said they wowld doe they
    have done
In making pore and ritch mens estate all one;
The rytch no rent, the pore their howses gett,
The ritch no mony have, the poore no meat ...
Woe worth the while what shall become of mee
When poore and ritch are thus in one degree.

Economy and environment

Economic problems highlighted in the petition of 1452 did not evaporate with the arrival of the Tudor Age. The withdrawal of the cloth industry was already significant before 1485 and the city came increasingly to rely upon its role as a market centre for the neighbouring hinterland.

The cloth industry struggled on in the city for another century after 1485, but continued to decline. In 1581, of the 100 wealthiest people assessed for tax, only 9 were involved in the making, and only 2 in the retailing, of cloth. Retailing, food and drink trades, leatherworking

and metal crafts dominate the other 90 per cent or so of the taxable top hundred. The continuing problems of clothworkers dominate calls from the city to central authority for help in 1618, 1622 and 1631, by which time the marginally less poverty-stricken people of neighbouring 'hundreds' were called upon to pay relief for the clothworkers of The Soke. John Taylor, a traveller who visited in 1623 during these difficulties, though admittedly during the harvest in August, commented that he saw 'an ancient city, like a body without a soul ... I walked from one end of it to the other and saw not 30 people of all sorts'.

Transfer of property from religious to secular ownership was a key effect of the mid-sixteenth-century Reformation on Winchester. However, the idea that ecclesiastical communal ownership simply gave way to ownership by lay individuals would be wrong. Certainly this happened in the case of Hyde Abbey, whose lands passed via Thomas Wriothesley to the Bethell family, who had built a brick and stone mansion house on part of the site by 1570. Otherwise it was institutions, particularly the city government, that gained property from the dissolved religious houses, especially within the walls (**colour plate 9**). The city government in 1540 owned 109 properties (including 30 gardens), which generated 53 per cent of the corporation's income. By 1554 this number had increased to 183 (45 gardens) with a concomitant increase in income for the city. The city also inherited the sites of churches closed after the 1545 Act for the amalgamation of churches and classified as 'waste ground'. On the whole, in the century after 1450, property provided a significant proportion of the city government's income, which generally fluctuated between 40 and 60 per cent.

Economic links with the hinterland were a sufficient, if limited, base for the city's economy in times of peace in the sixteenth century. However, particularly during the Civil War of the seventeenth century, such links with the hinterland were easily broken. The Civil War was disastrous for the economy of Winchester. The market function, central to the economy of the city, was all but destroyed by the plundering of goods, carts and horses. The castle was cast down and Wolvesey destroyed.

Civil War: role and politics

Winchester was important strategically in the Civil War as a bastion astride the great west road between the royalist west and the parliamentary south-east. The oligarchy and the Church gave it royalist leadership in the early 1640s. Divisions within the local gentry and between Winchester burgesses were thrown into stark relief by the choice between king and parliament.

One Winchester burgess was Sir William Waller, a parliamentary commander who defeated a royalist garrison of the city in 1642 (and who allowed wholesale plundering of shops and general destruction). Another was Sir William Ogle, the chief royalist leader in the city. Ogle recaptured the city in 1643, was unable to prevent parliamentary looting for a second time in 1644 and was blasted out of the castle by Cromwell in 1645. Thereafter, the only overt connections to the war were the execution of a royalist who had plotted to 'spring' the king from imprisonment on the Isle of Wight and a loyalist address to the king as he made his final journey to London in 1648.

In 1651 a garrison was placed in the city to defend it against the threat of royalist resurgence inspired by the future Charles II. During the interregnum there was a diminution of trade and its market function was curtailed. The city government which had supported the king – and whose members had been much criticized as self-seekers by John Trussell early in the 1640s – was replaced in 1649 by a pro-parliament group. This regime held sway until the Restoration.

Religion and culture

Whatever the decayed state of the economy in the later fifteenth century, the Church survived in a stable but reduced state in the final years of the fifteenth and the first four decades of the sixteenth century.

A regular programme of building took place at the cathedral during the last half-century or so of its existence as a priory. Under bishops Courtenay (died 1492) and Langton (died 1501) and their contemporary priors, Hunton and Silkstede, there were works in both stone and wood at the east end – work in the Lady Chapel and in Langton's own chapel.

The embellishment of Langton's chapel by his successor, Fox, perhaps drawing on motifs from mainland Europe, was probably completed by 1510, and contained the first elements of Renaissance style in the city – among the earliest in England. This was followed by the construction of Fox's chantry chapel in 1513–18. Apparently originally entirely Gothic in its design by Thomas Vertue, the king's master mason, Renaissance elements crept in during construction.

The main achievements of Bishop Fox's time (1501–28) were the walling in of the presbytery and the provision in 1525 of Renaissance chests for the remains of Saxon worthies, now atop those walls. Both the presbytery walls and Fox's chantry chapel are built of Caen stone, imported via Southampton, and are, bar the detail, fine testimony to the final flourish of the Gothic at Winchester.

All this remains today. But adjacent to the Fox chantry stood the great shrine of Swithun of 1476. Destruction of this focus for pilgrims for nearly half a millennium was concluded at 3 a.m. on the morning of Saturday 21 September 1538. Silver valued at £1320, according to Wriothesley who oversaw the dismantling, was the main precious metal recovered. In 1539 the priory was dissolved and in March 1541 the new foundation of Dean and Chapter was established by letters patent. Within the cathedral the new foundation was celebrated with a series of woodcarvings on the dean and chapter's stalls. The chapter consisted of twelve prebendaries, some of whom, like Dean Kingsmill, were recruited from the former brothers.

The destruction of Swithun's shrine and the Dissolution of the monasteries not only had major economic effects but also topographic effects on Winchester. The cathedral priory, Nunnaminster (57), Hyde Abbey and all the friaries disappeared. Many buildings were demolished straight away,

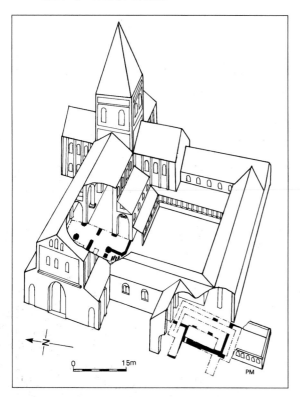

57 *Reconstruction of Nunnaminster showing late medieval phases revealed by excavation and the scale of the building in the later Middle Ages. Eadburh's shrine was below the nave excavations shown here. Plans from limited excavations have been used to re-create a major structure (after Winchester Archaeology Office; redrawn by Philip Marter).*

for example Hyde, whence stone, timber, slates, iron and glass from the church, cloister, chapter house, dormitory, frater, the hall and lodgings were taken for the king's use.

Like the city corporation, Winchester College also profited, gaining principally the lands of the Dominican and Franciscan friaries in the north-east sector of the walled city and certain lands beyond the walls derived from friary, chapel and chantry foundations. Away from the built-up area of the city the dean and chapter and the bishop retained their lands (see **colour plate 9**).

At the cathedral, the change from a priory to a regime based on a dean and chapter required adjacent property for the new prebendaries. Thus the old prior's lodging was preserved as the Deanery, which it still is today. This building retains its impressive late medieval timber roof over the hall. Other significant survivals from the priory include a part of the kitchen (now incorporated in 10 The

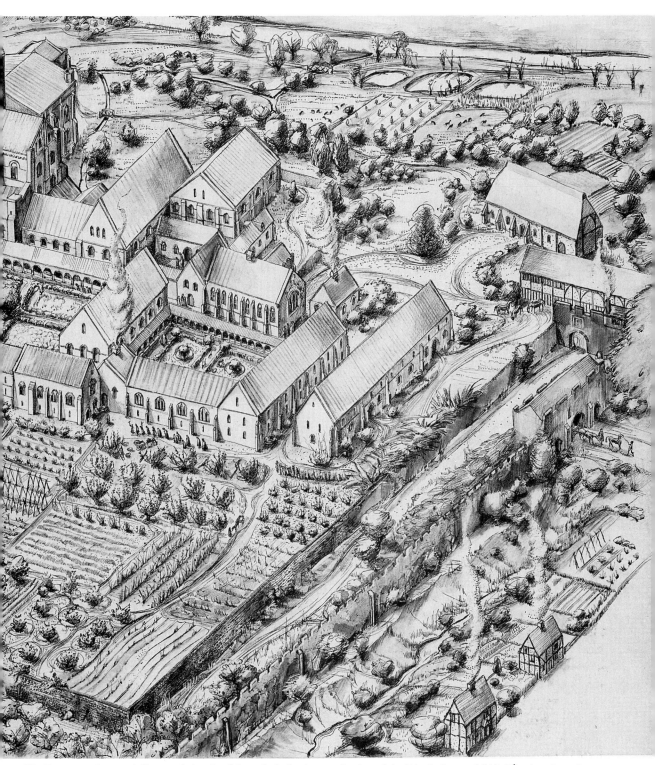

58 *Reconstruction, specially commissioned, of the cathedral priory at the time of the Dissolution, c. 1540. The drawing takes account of the surviving architectural fragments of the priory, results of excavations at St Mary in the Cemetery (left) and documentary research (drawn by Judith Dobie, English Heritage).*

Close), the Norman pillars of the chapter house beside the south transept, and two notable timber-framed buildings: the 'Pilgrims' Hall' (probably the priory guest-house) of *c.* 1300, and the stables (*c.* 1500) in the south of The Close (**58**).

The decline in the number of parish churches had slowed down in the fifteenth century, but the first half of the sixteenth century saw the closure of a further 11 out of the 57 of 1148. Bishop Fox carried out a rationalization programme which closed most of this group, including St Mary in Tanner Street. St Mary has been thoroughly excavated and the results show a building of flint rubble with some chalkwork, but, so far as is known, it had little expensive ashlar work. Two churches, St Mary in the Cemetery (fragments of which survive to the west of the cathedral) and St Stephen, were closed as a direct result of the Reformation. Some of the once grand churches of Winchester disappeared at this time, for example St Mary Kalendar (on the north side of the High Street opposite the east end of The Pentice), which was probably in ruins by 1554 when it was granted to the city.

Some positive developments in parish churches did occur. In 1527 the wealthy suburban church of St John in the Soke was given seventeen 'messuages and quitrents', which added to its secure financial base founded on wealth from the St Giles Fair.

For the most part the century between the Reformation and the Civil War saw a continuing decline in both the decoration and the numbers of ecclesiastical buildings in the city. Renaissance style, particularly in the context of the reformed Church, was less given to statuary than the Gothic of previous centuries. This is most strikingly seen in the contrast between Bishop Fox's chantry of 1513–18, which has fifty-five groined niches, and Bishop Gardiner's chantry of *c.* 1556–8, which has just three.

Royalty and bishops: 1550–1640

Among the reasons why Winchester was an appropriate place for the marriage of Mary Tudor to Philip of Spain in 1554 was its associations with her uncle, Arthur, and his wife,

Katherine of Aragon, who was, of course, also Mary's mother. The chair in which Mary is said to have sat during her marriage can be seen in the cathedral today.

Gardiner, bishop in 1531–51 and again in 1553–5, confronted an uncertain future during the Reformation. A chapel established after his death by his successor, Bishop White, was intended as a chantry. But there is some doubt that it was ever completed – and it was the last such structure to be built in the cathedral. White's tenure was short: he was deprived of his bishopric and sent to the Tower.

Fragments of a remarkable Renaissance tomb of 1559 in the cathedral, which share ornamental features with Gardiner's chapel, have recently

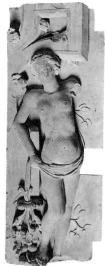

59 *Tomb of Thomas Mason (died 1559). Fragments of this tomb, a cartouche 86 by 28cm (34 by 11in) and its male and female supporters c. 87 by 34cm (34 by 13in) are now in the Triforium Gallery. With Gardiner's chantry these were the only pieces of High Renaissance work in the cathedral (photograph and copyright: Winchester Research Unit).*

been reconsidered. This was the tomb, now largely destroyed, of Thomas Mason, whose father, Sir Robert, had been lay dean of Winchester from 1549 to 1554 (**59**). However, not until the 1630s is the Renaissance theme once more taken up in the cathedral in the light of James I and Charles I's liberalization of religion. The fine screen by Inigo Jones (now destroyed) adorned by bronze figures by Le Sueur was the most significant element of the return of the Renaissance style which placed Winchester Cathedral 'once more in the forefront of English artistic endeavour' (Martin Biddle).

Undistinguished wooden portrait sculptures of kings James I and Charles I adorned the corners of the choir vault for almost two centuries from *c.* 1635. These effigies survived the Civil War probably through their inaccessibility, but quantities of lead recovered from them after they were taken down suggest they may have been used for target practice by soldiers in the Civil War in a vain attempt to dislodge them (**60**).

The destruction wrought by the war, on the city and on the cathedral, was very considerable. Certain of the mortuary chests from Fox's screen were entirely destroyed, others severely damaged by acts of iconoclasm, which cut at the very roots of the discredited monarchy. Documents from the cathedral library were allowed to blow about unheeded. Some treasures such as the Arthur tapestries from 1486 were saved in Winchester College, but in terms of statuary, stained glass, fittings and documents the cathedral was

60 *This cathedral roof-boss of Charles I and Henrietta Maria was, like the portrait sculptures, out of reach of the Cromwellians (photograph: John Crook).*

wrecked as never before or since. The great twelfth-century Bible survived both Reformation and Civil War: it was saved precisely because it contained the Scriptures, the rock on which the reformed faith was founded. During the interregnum the cathedral, like the city, lay quiet, awaiting whatever the future might bring.

8

'A great deal of good company'

1660–1800

Winchester had fewer inhabitants for much of the late seventeenth and eighteenth centuries than in earlier periods. But the quality of life for those who remained there, where it can be tested, was comfortable and varied. Royal interest, exemplified by the planning and building of Charles II's palace on the site of the medieval castle, was both preceded and accompanied by a flurry of high-status housing for clergy and courtiers. Probate inventory evidence suggests that a relatively small number of Winchester residents lived in real comfort enjoying clocks, mirrors, leather armchairs and feather beds. This group included clergy, wealthy merchants and that elusive group who were termed 'gent.' – not necessarily by themselves, but more significantly by their peers, who drew up the probate documents.

Thus a townscape of large and well-appointed residences emerged. The rebuilding of Wolvesey Palace by bishops Duppa and Morley after the Restoration followed the return of a resident bishop after the Civil War. The rebuilding drew on the ruins of the neighbouring medieval palace as a readily available quarry. Great houses in The Close for the clergy developed; at first drawing on the available stone from the demolished conventual buildings as used at 9 The Close, then in brick, for example at numbers 1 and 11.

Available space within and outside the walls was in demand for building large houses for courtiers at the time of Charles II's palace, and in the years following his death. The great houses were set in estates, some behind gates, such as

Penton's House (**colour plate 10**); others boasted heraldic devices such as those, now to be seen in Victoria Road, from Essex Paulet's house on the site of Hyde Abbey. The eighteenth century saw a continuation of grand building, with red-brick mansions both within the walled area and in the suburbs, although the city walls were increasingly insignificant.

Visitors were divided about what they thought of the older monuments, though there were positive comments on the new grand houses. Some eighteenth-century visitors criticized the old timber-framed buildings (above, pp. 14–15). Plenty of fine seventeenth- and eighteenth-century domestic architecture is to be seen in the city. A good proportion of this is on a small scale, and provided dwellings for those who served and administered the large residences. Cottages with brick frontages, such as those in Canon Street, are often adaptations of earlier buildings, and incorporate timber frames behind their brick façades.

In High Street premises such as Jacob and Johnson's *Hampshire Chronicle* offices, and elsewhere in the city, for example in Kingsgate Street, there are bow windows, which some contemporaries saw as indications of shameful exhibitionism by people who wished to be seen! Where enlarged windows were added to medieval properties, for example at The Pentice in the High Street, there must also have been another motive – to provide additional light. The city boasts some eighteenth-century doorcases, with particularly good examples in St Thomas Street and St Peter Street.

Population and society

The hearth tax of 1665, one of a series of ingenious taxes designed to raise money for a government with grand ideas but little ready money after the Civil War, provides a basis for estimating a population of some 5900 in Winchester. The Compton religious census of 1676 (to discover numbers of Conformists, Nonconformists and Catholics) gives a somewhat lower figure of 3700. The hearth tax gives some clues to wealth distribution, or lack of it, in the city: 25 per cent of the households within the walls together with the eastern suburb were exempted on the grounds of poverty.

The difference in figures between 1665 and 1676 may reflect a genuine decline in population in the decade. The effects of the 1666 plague on the city were sufficiently severe for a decline of 25 per cent to be recorded in excise totals for the city between September 1666 and March 1667 (**61**). The 1668 hearth tax commissioners cited Winchester as a city where plague had led to a decline in receipts.

Bishops' visitation returns in 1725 and 1788 provide useful indications of population size in this least-studied period of the city's history. Enumeration by incumbents of numbers living in their parishes in 1725 add up to just over 4000, of which 2758 lived in the parishes within the walls. This hints at a rise in the population of the suburbs. The incomplete returns for 1788 suggest an overall decline perhaps to between 3500 and 4000. There is no clear trend in 1788 of growth in the suburbs contrasting with decline within the walls.

Society in the city continued to be dominated by clergy, gentry and more briefly courtiers. Daniel Defoe liked most of what he found c. 1725:

> here is a great deal of good company; the abundance of gentry being in the neighbourhood, it adds to the sociableness of the place. The clergy also here are, generally speaking, very rich and very numerous. As there is such good company, so they are gotten into that new-fashioned way of conversing by assemblies.

However, he was critical of what he discovered of St Cross where the brothers were not 30 in number as he had expected but only 14, while the master lived in the style of the best gentlemen – a matter of complaint 'when public charities, designed for the relief of the poor are embezzled and deprecated by the rich to the support of luxury and pride'.

61 *Detail of the plague monument outside West Gate. Plague disappeared from Winchester after a final serious outbreak in 1666 (photograph: John Crook).*

Restoration and politics

The Restoration of 1660 was on the whole popular in Winchester and was in time to prove significant for the development of the city as we know it today. There was pain mixed with pleasure in 1662 when reforming commissioners ejected the 1649 city government on the grounds of disloyalty. Charles II granted a charter confirming previous reductions of the city 'fee farm', or annual sum of compounded royal dues paid by the town to central government. At this time Charles gave the city the great Lely portrait of himself which hung for many years in St John's Rooms on The Broadway (see **5a**), but now can be seen in the Guildhall.

Royal patronage was a two-edged weapon, for in 1684 Charles II called in the city's governing charter and refused to reissue it. Such relief as was felt at King Charles's death was short lived as James II left the city without a charter until September 1688 when he forced his own nominees on to the powerless corporation under the guise of reissuing a medieval charter. Ten weeks later in early December James, in desperate straits, reinstated the city's privileges and with them an Anglican council led by Thomas Wavell; soon afterwards the king was rejected by the country at large in the Glorious Revolution.

Restoration and rebuilding

On their return to the city after 1660, successive bishops found much needed to be done. Brian Duppa began rebuilding at Wolvesey. His successor George Morley built enthusiastically: between them they spent £4000 on the bishop's palace. Morley also created the eponymous Morley College for clergy widows in 1674 on part of the vacant New Minster site to the north of the cathedral. It was at this time that another institution, Winchester College, began to modernize some of its building stock after some 350 years. The 1680s witnessed the building of the imposing 'School', for commoners.

The Restoration brought a spate of repair and building in the city. As Schellinks saw in 1662 (p. 13), the city walls were breached and the castle slighted. Wolvesey, once the greatest Romanesque house in England, had, in the words of Defoe, 'been ruined by that known church incendiary, Sir William Waller, and his crew of plunderers'. Elsewhere, buildings in the city had simply fallen into disrepair. Such was the case with the church of St Peter in Macellis on St George Street, which had not been a place of worship for at least a century before the

Restoration and had become a collection of ruined walls being 'no other than a very dunghill, a place of all manner of excrements and a loathsome, noisome nuisance to the parts of the city adjoining it'. This church was excavated in the 1950s (p. 50).

Depopulation and decline left spaces in the city, but even in 1662 the High Street was in good order: 'the largest and best street for shops and houses,' commented Schellinks. These included Sir Robert Mason's great Eastgate House, which boasted sixteen hearths in 1665, and dominated the area north-east of the High Street, formerly occupied by two friaries. Across the road, Abbey House flourished on the site of St Mary's Abbey. There were altogether a dozen houses each with the large sum of ten hearths which, while not a certain indication of wealth in every case, helps to define this group of large houses in the city. This group was swelled by canons' houses in The Close – there were nine such houses recorded with ten hearths in 1674.

The Caroline palace and its lands

After attending the races at Winchester in 1682 Charles II decided to create an English Versailles in the city. He commissioned plans for an extensive palace on the medieval castle platform. The following year the foundations were laid and the building began to rise imposingly. The death of the king in 1685 halted the works (**62**). James II showed no interest in the project. The 138ha (342 acres) which had been acquired within and without the city for the project – partly for a grand vista from the palace to the cathedral – were blighted and building activity in the city declined for a time due to uncertainty about the future.

In time the land began to seep on to the market and the group of large red-brick houses was extended in the remaining part of the century and expanded in the eighteenth century. In 1705 there were twenty substantial houses in the city. Many of these large red-brick houses survive today both within the city and without the walls. Among those from the seventeenth century are 26/27 St Swithun Street (1680s), possibly originally built

62a *Charles II's palace, as it was eventually completed after his death, lacked much of the fine detail of Wren's design. The upcast of the Norman castle mound is seen in the foreground. The castle hall is to the right (Author's collection).*

for James II when Duke of York; Avebury House (1692), St Peter Street (for the Duchess of Portsmouth); Hyde House in the northern suburb; Abbey House, of which only one wing now survives (for William Pescod, Recorder of the city). From the early eighteenth century fine examples include Serle's House and the former Southgate Hotel, Southgate Street, both probably from the second decade of the century (see **3**).

William Godson's measured map published in 1750 is the major cartographic source for the city before the nineteenth century (**63**). An album of his drawings of much the same date and mar-

ginal drawings on the 1750 map of some of the major structures new, old and hypothetical are further valuable visual materials. The east prospect of the King's House appears as designed by Wren, and not in its incomplete form as built. Also drawn on the margin of the map are the old institutions – cathedral, college, Great ('County') Hall and market cross; almshouses – the old St John's on The Broadway and the new Morley College; and the town's centre of government – the new Queen Anne guildhall of 1714 (**64**). Finally some grand houses including Wolvesey Palace and large private houses in the city are seen, the whole creation dedicated to the lay authorities: the mayor, corporation and MPs of

62b *Remains of the palace after the fire of 1894 (WCM PWCM 2084).*

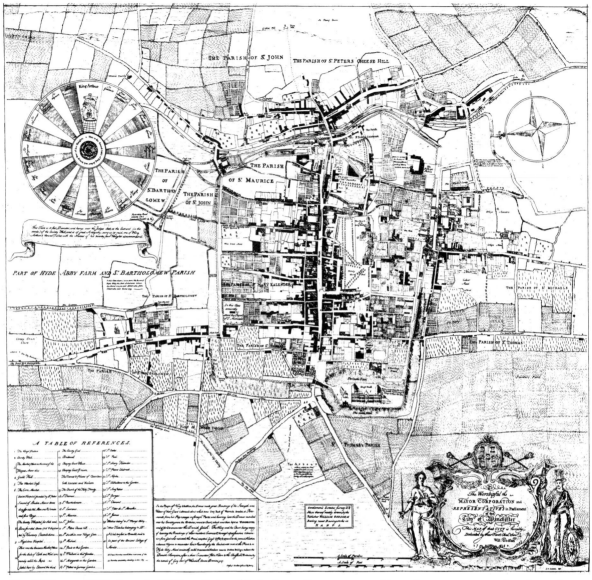

63 *1750 map of Winchester by William Godson (Author's collection).*

the city. The great clergy houses of The Close do not therefore appear.

Economy

Building was not the only economic activity taking place in the 150 years which followed the Restoration. There is evidence of transport coming to the city and affecting the environment. In 1691 horse teams were banned from parts of the High Street on market days; in 1713 Kingsgate Street was widened to protect pedestrians from heavily laden carts. In 1696 an estimated £20,000 worth of cheese was sold at the Magdalen Fair, which Celia Fiennes noted was a 'considerable' event drawing 'a vast many of waines from severall parts especially from the West Country'. She noted hops as a prime commodity at the fair and hopyards on the banks of the ruined castle, below the new palace.

Wealthy gentry and clergy brought business (**65**): in 1676 there were 76 licensed victuallers. Ten years later the city far outstripped other towns in the county in a survey of stabling and

64 *Queen Anne guildhall of 1714, redrawn from the sketch on Godson's map of 1750 (redrawn by Alejandra Gutierrez).*

was one of only six provincial towns in the country with stabling for more than 1000 horses. Plans were afoot as early as 1664 to put in place the Itchen navigation from Southampton to Winchester. In 1704, 90 shops were assessed within the walls.

The flurry of economic activity before 1700 was perhaps beginning to fail by *c.* 1725 when Daniel Defoe recorded of Winchester 'here is no manufacture, no navigation', although he found the society of the city agreeable. Thereafter there was, perhaps, a gradual improvement, most strikingly the creation of a silk-mill which employed 300 people by 1800 in the east of the walled area and, from the point of view of the building trades at least, the creation of a fine hospital and successive prisons.

Religion and culture

In 1721 it was remarked that the clergy occupied the best houses in Winchester. In 1735 four Cambridge gentlemen on tour noted the great reduction to nine of the number of parish churches. It was also noted that Morley's great palace at Wolvesey had run to ruin because, it was suggested, his successors perhaps thought it 'too magnificent for Apostolick Men to live in'.

In reality there were other factors, for the bishops in the eighteenth century were mostly older men, appointed to Winchester in their declining years, and who were not keen either to live there or to take an active role in the diocese: Willis was 60, Hoadly 58 and John Thomas 64. Brownlow North (died 1820), brother of the Prime Minister Lord North, was appointed in 1781 at the age of 40 and spent the second half of his life as Bishop of Winchester, but little of it in the city. He spent a good deal of time and money restoring Farnham Castle but at Winchester he demolished the south and east wings of Wolvesey.

Catholicism once more became a feature of the religious life of the city after the Restoration. A Catholic graveyard, still in existence beyond the West Gate, was opened soon after 1660 and James II was able to muster a Catholic city council in the dying days of his reign. Catholics made such a great financial contribution to the city that the mayor in 1720 refused to comply with a demand from the bishop to expel them. By 1800

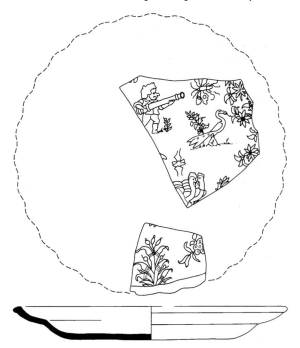

65 *Fragments of a faience plate made at Moustiers in southern France* c. *1760 and excavated from the garden of 24 St Thomas Street (after Matthews; redrawn by Alejandra Gutierrez).*

66 *The eighteenth-century Milner chapel, a fine Gothic Revival interior, and home of Catholic worship in the city (Author's collection).*

67 *Parchment Street Hospital. Founded in the eighteenth century, the hospital was at the end of its life when this picture was taken* c. *1865 (WCM PWCM 3625).*

not only were there Benedictine nuns established in St Peter Street and French priests at the former palace, but the fine Gothic Revival Milner Hall in St Peter Street (**66**) provided a new focus for the old religion in the city.

Politics and city government after 1700

In 1714 the city council was provided with a new guildhall centrally on the south side of the High Street. It is adorned with a statue of the donor, Queen Anne (see **64**); its curfew bell still sounds at 8 p.m. The eighteenth century was quiet in Winchester, which no doubt much commended itself to the citizens, compared to the upheavals, hopes and disappointments of the previous century. Corruption in politics and struggles between great county families, such as the Paulet dukes of Bolton (at Abbotstone and Hackwood) and the Brydges and Chandos (Avington), characterized the century. However, competition did provide certain spin-offs for the city, such as the clock on the Guildhall given by a Paulet in response to the gift of a statue of Queen Anne by a Brydges. Residents similarly vied with one another, both by building – such as Pescod and Penton either side of The Broadway – and by packing the council with freemen.

If the politicians of Winchester were not in agreement about what they did want for the city, they were agreed about what they did not want: disease (**67**), dirt (evidenced by the paving commissioners who began work in 1771) and a proposal for the establishment of a massive penal institution at the King's House (as an alternative to transportation), which was effectively opposed in 1785.

The eighteenth century closed with much evidence of an improved infrastructure for the city, which enabled Winchester to grow once more in the coming century. Essentials for the city to re-emerge as a populous county town were in place: a diverse retailing base, inns and alehouses and even, in silkweaving, a fledgling industrial activity.

9

'No one can build such places now'

1800–1900

Winchester grew in population in the nineteenth century: indeed, the city almost tripled in size. It underwent political reform after 1832, and saw the arrival of the first railway by 1840. This may have boosted the economy. The growth of Empire and the proximity of Southampton docks made the barracks a busy place. Hampshire was, for example, a prime base for the Zulu War of 1879 and at least one hero of that war is among those laid to rest in the West Hill cemetery. The Church of England was revitalized in Victoria's reign and the city was provided with a number of fine new churches, their Gothic Revival style echoing the medieval cathedral and Winchester College.

Population and society

In 1801 the first decennial census found 5826 people in Winchester, a substantial rise from the maximum estimate of 4000 for 1788. It was the emunerations of 10,732 in 1841 and 13,335 in 1851 which were the first figures to match the highest projection for the Middle Ages of 11,625. After 1850 the city grew steadily by between 500 and 1500 a decade to reach 17,179 in 1891.

Administration and politics

Winchester's role as a county town, where courts were held and prisons were sited, is clear after 1800: a 'New County Bridewell', as it was termed on a map of 1805, in the northern suburb at Hyde, was supplemented within the ancient walled area by the architect George Moneypenny's 1805 extension of the gaol in Jewry Street, which was

briefly renamed Gaol Street. This unenticing appellation was abandoned and 'Jewry Street' was revived in 1830. By 1850 another gaol was created on West Hill. This is still in use today. The Great Hall of the castle, where trials had long been held, was refenestrated by O.B. Carter *c.* 1850 together with the adjacent Grand Jury Chamber.

Winchester was rarely if ever at the centre of political reform, although the 1832 Great Reform Act forced the city to take action. Reforms worked through slowly, and from an architectural and administrative point of view the significant changes came towards the end of the century with the building of the great neo-Gothic guildhall adjacent to The Broadway in 1873 and with the creation of the Hampshire County Council in 1888, with offices based around the former castle site.

The railways

The London and Southampton Railway (later the London and South Western Railway), after nearly ten years of planning and building, opened in the city from Southampton in June 1839. Unparalleled earthworks were needed to bring the railway to Winchester from Basingstoke (opened 1840). Expensive though these works were, this main line from London was likely to be profitable, if any railway through Winchester was ever to be. There were some local investors, but on the whole the money came from London and from Manchester in particular, from the very heartland of the development of industrialization. The station was established at the north-west

68 *Didcot, Newbury and Southampton Junction Railway: cutting in progress at Chesil. The railway reached Winchester from the north in 1884 (HRO 85M88/13).*

corner of the old city defences, after an initial plan to drive the line through the old walled area near Staple Gardens had been defeated.

The economy and growth in size of the city led to the arrival of a second railway, the Didcot, Newbury and Southampton Junction Railway, whose Chesil Station in the eastern suburb opened in 1885. By coincidence, this was the year in which the sixth turnpike had been freed from toll in the city: five others had been freed and the tollhouses disposed of in the 1870s. However, financial and engineering problems, accompanied by acrimony and infighting, contributed to delays until 1888–9 when the extension of the railway across the flood plain of the Itchen to Shawford was achieved: there it joined the L.S.W.R. line to Southampton. Contemporary photographs show the major scale of the cutting and tunnelling which were required to create the railway in the area of Chesil Station (**68**). A brief period of com-

petition between railways and with horse-drawn transport ensued, but the first motor car was already on the streets of the city by 1900.

The economic effects of the railways on business and industry in the city await detailed analysis. However, it is plain to see in contemporary trade directories and newspapers that the railway enabled a growth in numbers of tourists who came to visit the city and other places nearby. Road transport, often provided by hotels and inns, met trains; printed guides and other publications, such as postcard views of the city, became readily available in the closing years of the century.

Georgian and Victorian buildings

In 1800 much of the city was devoid of inhabitants. Cole's map of 1805 shows large areas of the Brooks, north of the High Street, as gardens, with orchards on the western slopes within the walls. The northern, southern and eastern suburbs, however, were well stocked with properties but there is nothing much to the west. The brooks, which flowed along the middle of the three Brook streets, were open to the sky with a

69 *St John's Hospital, South. Owen Carter's lithograph of Garbett's buildings of 1833 (Author's collection).*

number of medieval timber-framed houses still standing adjacent to them, as Samuel Prout's well-known watercolour of 1813 shows.

This environment changed with ever increasing rapidity during the century. In particular the area of the Brook streets was developed beginning in the early years of the century as plots were bought up and tightly packed red-brick housing accommodated the increased numbers of inhabitants enumerated in the census. At the top end of the scale change was wrought by the creation of impressive buildings visible today, designed by a number of talented architects: the prison, Jewry Street, 1805 (Moneypenny); St John's Hospital and Almshouses, South, High Street, 1833 (Garbett) (**69**), and the Corn Exchange, now the library, Jewry Street, 1838 (O.B. Carter). Other works were by H.C. Browne (died 1853) and his son-in-law Thomas Stopher (died 1926).

Stopher created many buildings in brick and timber in the city, especially on corner sites – The Old Dolphin, High Street/St Thomas Street; The Talbot Inn, High Street/Staple Gardens; The Green Man, Southgate Street/St Swithun Street; The Crown and Cushion (now demolished), Jewry Street/North Walls; and many others including, notably, the De Lunn buildings in Jewry Street which show his lavish use of timber and steeply pitched roofs. The stone of the Gothic Revival churches of the early and mid-nineteenth century was followed by vernacular timbering, less authentic in its re-creation of medieval and early modern buildings than the church architecture.

Amenities

Winchester has always been plagued by dampness and poor drainage. It was these problems which led, for example, to the relocation of the hospital from Colebrook Street to Parchment Street in the eighteenth century. No real progress was made towards a solution to those difficulties until 1844, when the whole matter of drainage was opened up by the corporation's sanitary inspector and developed into the acrimonious 'muckabites' dispute in which the townspeople (who were ratepayers) opposed the improvements, while the institutions (exempt from rates) were in favour! Among the telling arguments adduced in support of proposals for change was that in well-drained towns life expectancy was 58. It was only 50 in Winchester and indeed in St Peter, Chesil, near the river in the eastern suburb, it was only 42.

Thirty years later, in the 1870s, the drains were improved and in 1875 a new sewage-pumping station at Garnier Road was opened (**70**). This pumped the sewage up on to St Catharine's Hill, thus alleviating problems in the city, although today sewage can still be smelled when the wind is in the east. Drainage was provided comparatively late.

In 1847 the Winchester Gaslight and Coke Company was formed, later called the Water and Gas Company following an Act of 1865. Residual buildings from the Gas Company's premises survive between the former Corn Exchange and Moneypenny's prison west of Jewry Street.

The railway to Southampton, opened in June 1839, cut off the downland to the west of the city, known as the West Hill. The isolation of this area was the trigger for the relocation of various amenities. The Winchester Cemetery Company was established there by Act of Parliament in 1840 to relieve the bursting city graveyards. O.B. Carter designed the Anglican and dissenting chapels (now demolished) and the extant blue-brick gatehouse. The prison moved to the West Hill *c.* 1850 and was joined by the hospital, designed by William Butterfield, in 1864–8 (**71**). Police headquarters, the Diocesan Training College (1862) and the gasworks were among other public enterprises which also moved there.

Institutional buildings

The great institutional medieval buildings, for example the cathedral and college, used local flint, or ashlar from a distance, for example Quarr stone from the Isle of Wight. Some of the stone used in post-medieval Winchester was reused non-local stone from the demolished monasteries, other ecclesiastical buildings and the medieval town walls and gates: a recycling of institutional stonework.

Among a range of diverse building materials already appearing in the city before the railway arrived were Portland stone and Exbury yellow ('white') bricks for the Corn Exchange (1838) in

70 *Garnier Road pumping station, opened in 1875, contributed to the alleviation of sewage problems in the city (WCM PWCM 9985).*

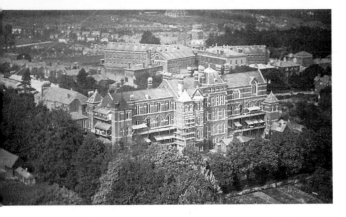

71 *The Royal Hampshire County Hospital and the star-shaped prison, both of the mid-nineteenth century (David Fry's collection).*

Both the mid-century prison and the workhouse were built to the cart-wheel plan, with a fine central watch-tower which still stands at the prison. The 'spokes', or wings, could be isolated for ease of control, and the prisoners (or poor!) driven to the extremities by the forces of order, reinforced from the hub.

Domestic and retail premises

The houses of the solid middle classes pretended to be stone by employing a stuccoed effect, incised to look like blocks, as at Medecroft, Sparkford Road, 1868 (**72**), and can be seen grouped in the private houses of Christchurch Road and at St Cross, or at the officer accommodation at St James Lane to the south of the city, and also along the west road, outside West Gate.

Jewry Street. Institutional buildings, where funds were available, used new stone, for example in the churches, at the Diocesan Training College (John Colson, 1862) and at the new guildhall (Jeffery and Skiller, 1873), which are noteworthy stone Gothic buildings of the later nineteenth century.

Red brick was retained for permanent residential institutions of middling and lower status, decorated or not according to function. Fancy diapered and patterned brickwork was employed by architects such as Garbett (St John's Hospital and Almshouses, South, 1833) and Butterfield (West Hill hospital 1860s). A new barracks was created in 1894 after fire almost irretrievably damaged the buildings of Charles II's palace (see **62b**) and provided an opportunity for rebuilding. Here, echoing the palace structure, the main medium was red brick, decorated with stone details preserved from the ruins. Although impressive to look at, the hill-top barracks was built cheaply with thin walls which let in the rain. The workhouse, now St Paul's Hospital, is significantly lacking in such architectural decorative distinction in its plain red brick, being the lowest grade institutional building.

O.B. Carter was employed for a variety of domestic projects subsequent to designing the Corn Exchange, some financed by institutions such as the St John's Charity who owned many sites in the city. His designs included Bath stone and yellow brick, for example at Clifton Terrace, which was begun during the 1840s and was still being built in 1851. At least one of Carter's designs, Chernocke Place, used black porphyry for internal details, perhaps the first imports of such stone into the city since Roman times.

The red brick which had enjoyed such social status in the century and a half after the Civil War lost its pre-eminence to stone and stonework effects – where the stucco merely masked the bricks! – and became the material of lower-status

72 *Medecroft, Sparkford Road, a spacious house in the southern suburb begun in 1868 only a hundred metres or so from the main railway line (right) (Author's collection).*

housing in the Brooks, where the poorest people lived, and for small-scale housing in blighted areas of the suburbs around the stations and goods yards, for example.

The suburbs, however, began to grow in the later nineteenth century, for example along Stockbridge Road which was realigned because of the railway; at Fairfield Road (where the builder went bankrupt in the mid-1890s), near the L.S.W.R. station; at Highcliffe near the Chesil Station, and to the north at Hyde where the properties were more substantial. In general the quality of the buildings improves the further they are from the stations. The cheapness of brick no doubt led to its almost universal adoption in business premises – breweries, factories, workshops and stables.

Economy

How did the growing population of Winchester earn a living? Major and continuing building works during the century provided employment for many people. The census of 1851 shows a significant number of bricklayers as heads of household. Colebrook Street, near the cathedral, chosen at random, provides a snapshot with several households headed by bricklayers. Associated trades such as carpentry and plumbing also feature. By contrast, the second half of the century saw a decline in the number of agricultural labourers, although this trend was in part due to the reclassification of occupations within the census after 1861. However, in the 1851 census, the first in which places of birth are given, the city shows a population with diverse geographical origins and in varied employment.

There was industrial activity in the city such as at a foundry in Colebrook Street in the 1850s, which was joined by Jewell's foundry in the Brooks from the 1870s. A number of breweries was established after 1850. These were located at the margins of the medieval walled area, such as St Swithun Street, St James Lane, Hyde Street and Eastgate Street. These locations, away from the High Street, were selected no doubt because land was available comparatively cheaply.

Trade directories and the census demonstrate the dominant service sector of the city's economy. In 1859 those registered in White's trade directory bear this out: 31 bakers, 27 grocers, 27 general shopkeepers and 25 butchers, were outnumbered by 33 bricklayers, 40 booksellers and 57 insurance offices. There were 10 banks. Professionals such as lawyers (there were 22 attorneys in 1859), clergy and army officers were numerous then and are still familiar in Winchester society.

The largest group of businesses in the city in the 1859 trade directory was some 120 establishments providing hospitality. These ranged from hotels to inns and taverns: about a quarter of them were beerhouses. This burgeoning hospitality industry catered for local people, country people coming to market and the ever-growing numbers of visitors. Earlier in the century, Cobbett had enjoyed a market-day dinner at The Swan with farmers and 'a great number of opulent yeomen', joined after the meal by gentlemen.

Religion and culture

There was an air of decay about the fabric of Anglican churches of Winchester in the early nineteenth century: at the beginning of the century there was a handful of medieval churches which, together with the fine eighteenth-century Milner chapel for Catholic worship (see **66**), were supplemented by Nonconformist chapels, examples of which were sited around the Brooks area, in Silver Hill (opened by John Wesley in 1785) and at Parchment Street (pre-1800). After the Emancipation Act of 1829 places of worship continued to become more numerous, for example by the addition of the chapel in Upper Brook Street (c. 1839). The Anglicans responded to Catholic emancipation with Holy Trinity, Upper Brook Street (1853), which was a High Church serving a poor parish.

In 1851 a national religious census was held, the only one ever to be carried out because, it is said, the census revealed that in the country as a whole there were many more Nonconformists than Anglicans at church on 30 March that year! The

73 *St Maurice church in the High Street, rebuilt in 1842 by Gover, but retaining some Romanesque features. Apart from the tower, it made way for Debenhams c. 1960 (WCM PWCM 4440).*

statistics are much debated. Were the returns accurate? Some places of worship, for example Winchester Cathedral, sent no returns; some parish clergy refused to count their congregations. However, recorded attendance in Winchester showed over 6000 Anglicans, over 1600 Nonconformists and 750 Roman Catholics from a population of some 11,500 in the Winchester parishes, which included Weeke and Winnall. Thus Anglicans with over 70 per cent of all church-goers in the Winchester census far outstripped their competitors, as might be predicted in a cathedral city, and went strongly against the national trend. There was, incidentally, at that time no synagogue and no church of the Latter Day Saints.

Church attendance by all denominations was thus over 70 per cent, 3 per cent above the county average. There are no returns for certain sizeable parishes such as St Peter Colebrook, which had a population of 604, and St Faith with a population of 892, although people from these

parishes attended elsewhere. The extent to which people attended more than once, when many places of worship recorded three services, cannot be judged. It has been argued, however, that the Anglican figures represent single attendance by parishioners: Nonconformists were more likely to attend more than once on Sunday!

The growing population of the city from 1801 to 1851 was matched by a rise in church attendance. The fine nineteenth-century ecclesiastical buildings surviving in the city bear witness to the enthusiasms of clergy and their congregations to provide sufficient and up-to-date accommodation for their religious needs.

As the century progressed, the medieval churches of the city and suburbs were renovated, such as the derelict church of St Bartholomew, Hyde, or rebuilt, such as St Maurice in the High Street (Gover, 1842) (**73**) and St Martin, Winnall (Coles, 1858). Old St Thomas, which gave its name to the street where it had stood for centuries, was demolished in 1845 amid vociferous protests from conservationists. New St Thomas west of Southgate Street was complete in 1846, with a tower finished in 1857. It was considered by the authoritative architectural writer Nikolaus

Pevsner (1967) to be the best Gothic Revival church in the city. The spacious St Thomas was supplemented by additional Anglican places of worship after 1850: Christ Church (1858), St Paul, Weeke (1873) and finally All Saints, Highcliffe (1890–8). By this time the churchbuilding movement was in decline and the bell-tower of All Saints was never completed.

These churches and chapels were built and decorated largely with stone, which ranged from flint with ashlar quoins, window reveals and decorations at Holy Trinity in the poor Brooks, to fine ashlar work at Christ Church in the wealthy and growing southern suburb.

Winchester's associations with Jane Austen, who died in the city in 1817 (**74**), and with John Keats, who was inspired by the watermeadows to write his poem 'To Autumn', the season of 'mellow fruitfulness', on visiting Winchester in 1819, are well known. Later in the century Anthony Trollope dwelt in his novel *The Warden* (1855) on the St Cross scandal in which the Reverend Francis North, fifth Earl of Guilford, was found since 1808 to have derived more than £300,000 from his corrupt tenure of the office of Master of the hospital. That he was appointed by his father, Brownlow North (bishop 1781–1820), who had himself been appointed to Winchester by his brother the Prime Minister, made the scandal worse. Francis North, one of a number of family and friends appointed by Brownlow North, also improperly held a canonry at the cathedral and two other livings in the diocese.

The cathedral in the first part of the century (**colour plate 11**) was in a poor state of repair and the acerbic William Cobbett, while he may not have been representative of general attitudes, no doubt spoke for many. After visiting a Sunday service at the cathedral in 1830 he wrote:

There is a dean, and God knows how many prebends belonging to this immensely rich bishopric and chapter: and there were at this service, two or three men and five or six boys in white surplices, with a congregation of fifteen women and four men! Gracious God!

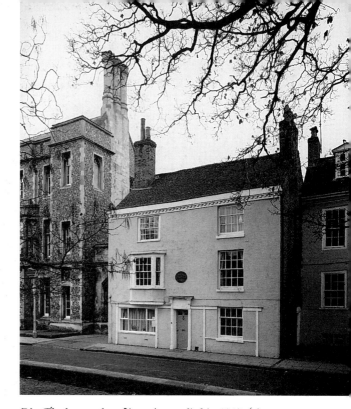

74 *The house where Jane Austen died in 1817 (photograph: John Crook).*

With such a start to the century in ecclesiastical affairs, matters could only improve. The appointment of the evangelical and youthful Charles Sumner as bishop in 1827 led to many changes. The chapter of the cathedral was reformed, and the training of teachers for the diocese was instituted with the foundation of the Diocesan Training College in 1840. The bishop's daughter-in-law, Mary Sumner, founded the Mothers' Union.

The great ecclesiastical buildings and the obvious antiquity of Winchester attracted numerous artists and subsequently photographers. Samuel Prout's view of Middle Brook Street (1813) has already been mentioned. G.F. Prosser (1805–82) lived in Winchester from 1852 and died in St John's Almshouses. He had published *Select Illustrations of Winchester* in 1833. Among his better-known views is the cathedral cemetery full of leaning tombstones (1849), before the stones were removed and the ground lowered after 1882. Beatrice Corfe (186?–1947), who lived in Chesil Street, was commissioned by the architect, builder and mayor Thomas Stopher to paint views of Winchester at the turn of the century. Among her output is a watercolour of the *Old pleasure fair in the Broadway* (1897) and remarkable interiors such as that, now in the possession of the Victoria and Albert Museum, of the wealthy Canon Valpy's beautifully furnished drawing-room *c.* 1900 (now a school dormitory) at 3 The Close.

Education

Beatrice Corfe was also an art teacher, and the censuses show numbers of art and music teachers as well as other school staff. The census convention for describing the majority of children as 'scholars' suggests an awareness of the growing importance of education – even if such appellations frequently do not mean that the children listed were studying!

Winchester College, which had languished in the eighteenth century, began to revive in the nineteenth. Especially under Headmaster George Ridding, who handed over to Dr Fearon in 1884, the college made great progress in modernization. Facilities such as the gymnasium (1875–80) hint at 'muscular Christianity' which was such a feature of the second half of the nineteenth century. By 1875 Winchester had already played Eton at cricket for nigh on half a century.

Education became more broadly based in the nineteenth century. The foundation of many parish and denominational schools, of which St Faith's survives as a school today, spread education down the social scale. Education for girls was provided by St Swithun's School, at 17 Southgate Street when it opened in 1884, but subsequently at North Walls where it remained until 1930. Peter Symonds College opened in 1897 as a school for boys aged 11–18 at 39 Southgate Street and moved to Owen's Road by 1899. In addition, a number of preparatory schools were founded in the late nineteenth century such as Westfield, later called West Downs, which occupied buildings created *c.* 1880 by the philanthropic Lord Northbrook for the Winchester Modern School, and set in generous playing fields. The school buildings and fields have recently returned to public educational purposes with their purchase, as a site for conference and student accommodation, by King Alfred's College.

The nineteenth century saw a transformation from a sleepy country town of some 5000 to a city of some 20,000 people, with a varied economy and society. A microcosm of the spirit of the age was that Charles Benny, a grocer, hotelier and Conservative politician, led the Winchester Cemetery Company, which in 1840 took over burial rights that the Church had monopolized in the city since Saxon times. As the nineteenth century gave way to the twentieth, Winchester was thriving demographically, economically and socially, with flourishing religious groups and with a broadening educational base.

10

Modern Winchester

from 1900

The twentieth century has been dominated by two world wars, and for Britain by retreat from Empire. To the west of the cathedral, where the Roman forum and the early Saxon royal palace once stood, there are two substantial war memorials. At Winchester College there is the peaceful war cloister; at King Alfred's College the Winton memorial chapel.

The military focus of the city has declined: the Russian gun from the Crimean War, the centre of a riot over proposals to remove it from the High Street in 1908, was quietly scrapped to supply the needs of the Second World War. A Boer gun from the South African war and a tank donated in return for generous support from Winchester people who purchased war bonds during the First World War have disappeared. The barracks has been sold for residential purposes, apart from residual military museums as monuments to the past. A new barracks outside the city at Flowerdown has less impact on the city.

Winchester is a centre of local government. At least one whole street, Westgate Street, was demolished for the building of the County Council buildings. Reorganization in 1974 brought the ancient boroughs of Southampton and Portsmouth under Hampshire County Council, though from April 1997 Southampton and Portsmouth become unitary authorities once more. The surviving railway station announces Winchester as the home of the Hampshire County Council. The district council has built new offices near the Guildhall and the cathedral,

with stores at Bar End and a Museum Service at Hyde. The finest building of recent years is undoubtedly the Hampshire Record Office, near the station, where the records of this most ancient city and the county are kept in purpose-built accommodation (**75**). This, together with the extensive programme of archaeology, which has been the theme of this book, epitomizes the late twentieth-century interest in the past of England in a post-imperial age. Links with Europe have strengthened economically, socially and with tourism – and the visitor can hardly fail to notice that the past of Winchester was shaped by Romans, Saxons and Normans.

Before 1918

In 1901 the city enjoyed celebrations for the millennium of the death of King Alfred (died 899), which should properly have been celebrated in 1899. The indefatigable mayor Alfred Bowker masterminded activities which culminated, so far as Alfred the Great was concerned, with the erection of Thornycroft's statue in The Broadway, and so far as Bowker was concerned, with the issue of a commemorative medal with his own image on one face and King Alfred's on the other!

The city appears a comfortable place in the Edwardian period. The many postcards of that era have views of bustling streets and sleepy suburbs. Trade directories show the arrival of multiple stores such as the Maypole Dairy, Boots and the International Stores. These new enterprises were strongly capitalized and had an

75 *The Hampshire Record Office, a fine modern building near the site of the medieval Hawkheye, and the north-western extremity of town walls (photograph: John Crook).*

impact on the ancient buildings of the city. Boots bought the Gudgeon arcade in The Pentice for over £4000 in 1903, demolished it and rebuilt on the site. Likewise, the International Stores chopped a building out of The Pentice and replaced it in 1909 with a structure with more storeys.

The increasing demands of traffic began to take a toll and led to the demolition of buildings for road-widening, a notable early example being at the corner of Chesil Street and Morn Hill, north of the Chesil Rectory (see **78**).

A threat to the cathedral from subsidence occurred early in the century. The great church was preserved by the strenuous efforts of William Walker, a diver who worked under the supervision of architects Colson and Jackson on the permanently flooded foundations to replace the medieval wooden 'raft' on which the cathedral was built with concrete. A significant change to the southern aspect of the cathedral resulted from the erection of (individually sponsored) buttresses, which encroached on the area of the pre-Reformation cloister.

King George V visited Winchester on St Swithun's day 1912 on the occasion of a service in celebration of the completion of the cathedral repairs. A commemorative card stated that this was the first official visit by a reigning monarch since Queen Anne – nearly two centuries before.

Winchester proved a suitable venue for a major international gathering of military attachés in 1910, based at the George Hotel. The Great War brought many soldiers to the city for training and in transit, and some who died were laid to rest in the West Hill cemetery. Prisoners of war were imprisoned on Winnall Down on the site of the medieval leper hospital.

Population

In the course of the twentieth century the city has continued to grow in size, from over 20,000 in 1900 to over 30,000 by 1971, a figure which has been more or less sustained since then. The rise has not by any means been regular during the century. By 1911 it was 23,378 and was 403 higher in 1921; in 1931 down to 22,970. There was no census in 1941 but by 1951 the figure had risen to 25,721, although this reflects boundary changes in 1932–5. The population continued to rise steadily: 28,770 in 1961 and 31,107 in 1971. Boundary changes in the 1970s led to a decline to 29,337 in 1981. In 1991 the population had crept up again to 29,758.

Social conditions between the wars

Some 460 citizens of Winchester gave their lives in the First World War. In the city, as elsewhere, the period following the Great War saw improved residential accommodation for the poorer people whose families had been so mutilated by war. In 1919 the city council Housing Committee declared that Winchester was almost entirely a residential area.

Winchester in the 1920s, although crowded in comparison with its past history, was not crowded by twentieth-century urban standards. Persons per acre in Winchester were computed at 12.3 for the 1921 census, compared with 17.5 at Southampton and 31 at Portsmouth. The outstanding response to the need for working-class housing was the Stanmore estate, truly homes fit for returning heroes to live in. The houses at Stanmore were provided with parlours, but only after a national debate which was fuelled by fears that talking might lead to insurrection! Plans of

Stanmore were displayed at the Wembley Exhibition of 1922 as a model estate. Female employment in the city was comparatively high at 33 per cent of the work-force in 1921, one element in this being the remarkable figure of 68 per 1000 women who were in personal service. This employment structure corresponded to the social and economic make-up of the city, with army, clergy, lawyers and the medical profession well represented.

The 1926 General Strike affected Winchester, where a small Labour movement confronted the Conservative authorities, and where by contrast some students from the Training College went to Southampton docks to unload ships during the nine-day stoppage.

Housing spread westwards from Stanmore Lane towards Battery Hill while, to the south-east of the city, 300 houses were added to Highcliffe in 1926–7. The changing population of this comparatively affluent city was catered for by an increasing number of multiple stores which proliferated between the wars, including Woolworth's (1929) and Marks and Spencer (1935), both of which developed sites on the north side of the High Street.

76 *The bypass built in the 1930s, designed to relieve the traffic bottleneck at Winchester. It was then one of only a handful of dual carriageways in the country and therefore dubbed 'one of Britain's most modern roads' (Kate Brooker/Author).*

The steady development in building of the 1920s, as exemplified by the Catholic church of St Peter (completed 1928) and the new St Swithun's School for girls (completed 1930), reflected liberalization of attitudes to Catholics (the Italians were on the allied side in the Great War) and to women who had contributed so much to the war effort, and who had finally achieved equal voting rights with men in 1928. The 1920s were comparatively prosperous and hopeful.

But the crash of 1929 hit institutional as well as individual fortunes. The Church suffered financially and lay institutional building virtually dried up in the city when the council buildings outside West Gate to the south were completed in 1932. It is significant in this respect that although designs for the great County Hall to the north of West Gate were prepared in the 1930s by Cowles-Voysey, it was not built until 1959–60. The major building work of the 1930s was the bypass (**76**),

115

perhaps built with the prospect of war looming. If so, by carrying military traffic around the city, it may have saved Winchester from the destructive bombing which destroyed so many communication centres in the Second World War.

The Second World War to the present

A bomb fell at Hyde, but overall Winchester survived the Second World War comparatively unscathed. Afterwards, however, austerity bit deep and the city fell into disrepair. With returning prosperity in the mid-1950s building began again. The demands of the motor car became increasingly felt: street widening brought about the destruction of the George Hotel (now partly overlaid by Barclays Bank) in the High Street in 1956 and the closure of the West Gate to traffic in the 1960s. In 1958 a science block and New Hall at Winchester College were created and in the following year the council buildings designed before the war were completed and named Queen Elizabeth Court.

These developments were followed by a spate of building throughout the city: for example the Wessex Hotel in 1961–2, adjacent to the cathedral, which was one of the sites made available to the archaeologists, funded by the new prosperity. A key change which affected residents of the city from the 1960s onwards was the institution of an electric railway to London. Thenceforward there has been a service which reaches the capital before 9 a.m.: this enabled daily commuting for the first time and transformed employment opportunities for residents.

Since then building and development have become part of the life of the city: commercial premises in the city centre; an industrial estate at Winnall; major additions to housing stock at Badger Farm, Harestock, Oliver's Battery, Teg Down, Weeke and Winnall. The last major buildings erected in the city were The Brooks Centre completed in 1991 (77) and works at the hospital. The clearance of sites brought about by these works has been the spur for much of the excavation of early Winchester, which is described above. At the end of the 1980s Winchester was dubbed the wealthiest city in Britain: a packed

77 *The Brooks Centre, a major shopping development completed in 1991 (photograph: John Crook).*

station car-park each morning bore witness to the exodus to work in London at that time. The 1990s are more uncertain, however.

Winchester became synonymous with the long-standing battle to save Twyford Down from destruction in a bypass project (**colour plate 12**). Although the Down was not ultimately saved, the long campaign contributed to a reconsideration of government transport policy on road building, sustaining Winchester's place on the national stage. It is no coincidence that throughout its existence the city has been a focus for routes, for the majority of the period seeking to exploit its position on the north–south route in the Itchen valley and the east–west route along the downs, but in recent years it has sought to avoid the fumes and noise of modern transport.

The future of Winchester's past

Key matters remain for investigation by present and future archaeologists of Winchester. They can be highlighted by period. The pre-Iron Age needs further examination. For the Iron Age, the relationship between St Catharine's Hill, the Oram's Arbour site and the surrounding countryside need exploration. The end of the Iron Age and the coming of the Romans needs elucidation. Was there a clean break or continuity of settlement? Was the market of the Belgae a folk-memory or a going concern after the invasion in AD 43? What are the connections between the villa-culture of the hinterland and the early Roman city, and subsequently?

The earliest Roman activities remain mysterious. Was there a fort and if so where? What was the sequence of the earliest Roman settlements in the city? From the Roman period key monuments remain undiscovered, unrecognized or unexcavated; the basilica in the forum, the Roman theatre and Roman baths are examples. There is a lack of information on Roman religion, for example on temples in Venta. There is also much more to be learnt about the end of Roman Winchester. To what extent did Roman remains, other than the earthworks of the walls, remain upstanding in the post-Roman period?

For the Saxon period the issues begin with the question of continuity, or lack of it, from the Roman past. There appears to be a cessation in activity within the walled area in the early fifth century. Do the cemeteries of Roman date and post-Roman date which contain, for example, decapitated bodies, indicate a continuity of anything other than violence? If there was continuity, what was its nature, and who were the power-brokers? Were they resurgent British or immigrant warriors? What is the relationship between the cemeteries around the city and Winchester itself in the early Saxon period and were there early churches adjacent to early Christian burials, for example in the later seventh century?

In later Saxon Winchester there are gaps, for example an increasing amount is known about Viking and Scandinavian influences on the city but artefactual evidence is at present scarce.

Saxon domestic housing awaits further analysis and interpretation. None the less, broadly speaking, the development of Saxon England can be charted through the archaeology of the city.

We now know much about medieval Winchester, but await, for example, a definitive pottery sequence. Certain major sites such as the royal palace and leper hospital remain to be investigated. From the eleventh century onwards the survival of documentation facilitates quantification, and analysis by occupation and status of population and society. The contribution of below-ground archaeology and the study of standing remains together with the documentary evidence combine to give, for Winchester, an especially detailed and integrated account of social archaeology and social history.

Post-Reformation Winchester is comparatively less well studied, but none the less much has been achieved in the last thirty years or so, starting with Tom Atkinson's *Elizabethan Winchester* (1963), which was followed by Adrienne Rosen's doctoral thesis on the society and economy of the city in the sixteenth and seventeenth centuries (1975).

Nikolaus Pevsner's *Hampshire* (1967) in the Buildings of England series, although now somewhat outdated on the medieval city, made an especially important contribution in listing many post-medieval buildings. He grouped by period, from their exteriors, the great red-brick houses from the period of the Restoration and eighteenth century and offered dates for certain of them.

The city has enjoyed a period of extensive excavation since the Second World War. Much of the information from these excavations is slowly coming to light through publication and through exhibitions and lectures. The bulk of the excavations remain to be published, which makes this account really no more than an interim report. However, the major monuments continue to attract visitors to the ancient capital of England as they have done for a thousand years and more. A walk through the city reveals a treasure-house of architecture of all periods set in riverine parks and a glorious chalkland landscape.

Glossary

Antonine(s) Roman emperors from Antoninus Pius to Commodus, AD 138–92.

Atrebates A tribe who settled in pre-Roman southern England.

bishopric pipe roll The annual account and manorial roll for the estates of the bishops of Winchester.

Brooks, the North-eastern quarter of the city, so called because of the brooks or water courses, now covered over, which run down Upper, Middle and Lower Brook Street (now Tanner Street). The Brooks excavations (1987–8) investigated an area between Middle and Upper Brook Street.

burh An Anglo-Saxon defended settlement.

chi-rho First two Greek letters of Christ, used as a Christian symbol.

Close, The Area surrounding the cathedral. To the south and east is the Inner Close where the post-Conquest monastery stood. This is still closed at night. To the north and west is the Outer Close, where Old and New Minsters were located.

dendrochronology The science of dating timber by analysis of tree rings to give a date when timber was felled, often coterminous with first use when used green.

Flavian(s) Roman emperors from Vespasian to Domitian, AD 69–96.

gild merchant Originally a body of merchants which in the Middle Ages became synonymous with town government (and which included non-merchants).

hide A measure of land notionally about 120 acres (49ha).

Hospital of St John A charitable foundation of which some medieval buildings survive north of The Broadway. Substantial additional buildings were added to the south of The Broadway in 1833. Series of almshouses are found at both locations.

illumination The embellishment of a manuscript with colour.

insula A rectangular area within a notional grid laid over a plan of the city identified by number beginning with Roman I at the forum and working outwards towards the walls.

long-and-short-work A characteristic of Saxon stone building in which corners were reinforced by stones laid with the long sides alternately upright and horizontal.

machicolations Openings in military architecture between corbels supporting a parapet, through which missiles could be thrown on attackers.

PPG 16 Planning Policy Guidance. Department of the Environment planning advice which addresses the integration of archaeology into the planning process.

Purbeck marble A shelly limestone (and therefore not a true marble) from Dorset, which takes a high polish.

samian ware A fine-fabric pottery of first to third century AD, usually red with decoration.

Soke, The Areas of the southern and eastern suburbs under the jurisdiction of the bishop, from 'soke', i.e. a local jurisdiction. Also the name of a large house in Chesil Street.

spolia Statuary etc. taken from ancient civilizations used to decorate medieval buildings.

staple A principal market or measuring place for a particular commodity, for example wool, as in Staple Gardens.

tarrage From the French *terre,* i.e. a land tax.

tesserae Small square/cubical pieces used to make mosaic pavements.

tufa Porous calcareous stone.

visitation returns Answers by clergy to standard sets of questions issued by bishops as 'visitors' of parishes.

Wolvesey Orginally Wulf's Isle, an area within the south-eastern quarter of the city, long occupied by the bishop's residence.

KING ALFRED'S COLLEGE
LIBRARY

A tour of the city

(Numbers in italics refer to the map on p. 120.)

Begin at the Tourist Information Centre in the Guildhall *(1)*, The Broadway *(78)*.

Leaflets are available and monument opening times can be checked. Tours are available with qualified guides twice daily Easter to October, Saturday mornings in the winter.

Thereafter start with the cathedral. Apart from the building itself visit the Triforium Gallery and cathedral library to see in particular the Winchester Bible. Outside the cathedral to the north look at the display which shows the development of Old Minster *(2;* see **22**). To the south note the remains of the monastic buildings (see **58**), the Deanery (medieval prior's lodging), the 'Pilgrims' Hall' with its timber roof of *c.* 1300 and the fifteenth-century stables by the gate *(3)*. Passing out of the Prior's Gate *(4)*, the adjacent King's Gate with its little church over it is of interest.

Left under the gate along College Street takes you past the house *(5)* where Jane Austen died (see **74**) to Winchester College *(6)* (10.00–13.00, 14.00–17.00; tours April–September) with its fourteenth-century Chamber Court, chapel and with the remarkable statue of the Virgin Mary over the Outer Gate. Beyond the college on the left is Wolvesey Palace *(7)* rebuilt incorporating the medieval chapel in the late seventeenth century. This is the home of the bishop. Beside it are the remains of medieval Wolvesey (April–September 10.00–18.00; October 10.00–16.00). Beyond Wolvesey follow the high wall round into The Weirs gardens beside the river, rerouted here by the Romans, a fragment of whose wall can be seen preserved towards the City Bridge end of the gardens *(8)*.

At the City Bridge visit the City Mill *(9;* April–September 11.00–16.45; March and October, Saturday and Sunday 12.00–16.00, National Trust) and pass into the High Street by way of St John's Almshouses, South *(10;* see **69**), which have '1833' in the east gable. Across the road are the north almshouses with their hall and chapel. The Thornycroft statue of King Alfred *(11)* dominates the High Street and has the Abbey Gardens beside it *(12)*. This was the site of medieval Nunnaminster (see **57**) where part of the structure can be seen displayed immediately west of the Guildhall. In the gardens is Abbey House now the mayor's offices and also the Abbey Mill with its fine portico *(13)*.

In the High Street, nos. 33 and 34 (see **46**) are intact medieval structures under The Pentice *(14)*. The Buttercross (see **48**) and adjacent Spinning Wheel are medieval *(15)*. Behind the Spinning Wheel is St Lawrence church and the City Museum *(16;* April–September, Monday–Friday 10.00–17.00; Saturday

10.00–13.00, 14.00–17.00, Sunday 14.00–17.00, closed on Mondays October to March) is nearby adjacent to The Close at the west end of the cathedral where the Cathedral Visitor Centre offers refreshments and a shop. Allow over two hours for a guided tour such as this, which would include 20 minutes in the cathedral (but not, for example, the Triforium Gallery and cathedral library). Individuals would cover the ground more quickly, and could take in the West Gate and Great Hall (below) within two hours.

Resuming, to the north of the High Street is The Brooks where the Winchester Heritage Centre *(17;* Easter–October, Tuesday–Saturday 10.30–13.00, 14.00–16.30, Sundays 14.00–16.30) in Upper Brook Street provides video and photographic displays and information.

Up the High Street towards the West Gate, Godbegot House *(18)* on the north side is a fine timber-framed courtyard house with the site of the medieval church of St Peter marked out on the paving behind beside St George Street. Jewry Street, to the north of the High Street, contains the former County Gaol (1805); Corn Exchange *(19;* 1838, O.B. Carter, now City Library) and the Theatre Royal. To the south of the High Street, Southgate Street has several fine eighteenth-century buildings, including Serle's House, now the Hampshire Regiment Museum *(20)*, and also on the west side St Thomas church, arguably the best Gothic Revival church in Winchester *(21)*.

The medieval West Gate *(22;* includes museum open as City Museum but closed November to January inclusive) is at the top of the High Street. Adjacent on raised ground are ruins of a rounded tower and sally port of the castle, and the unrivalled thirteenth-century Great Hall *(23;* see **40**) (April–October 10.00–17.00, November–March 10.00–16.00). Behind the hall is a small reconstructed medieval garden. Beyond the castle hall are remains of Charles II's palace built into the Peninsula Barracks, an impressive brick structure of 1894, beside which are found further military museums (Royal Hussars, Light Infantry, Brigade of Gurkhas, Royal Green Jackets), entered from the medieval garden. From here it is an easy stroll back to the Guildhall in The Broadway where the tour began.

The suburbs

West

The western suburb contains the area of Oram's Arbour where major Iron Age discoveries have been made *(24;* see **12**). It is flanked to the west by the remains of a large twelfth-century

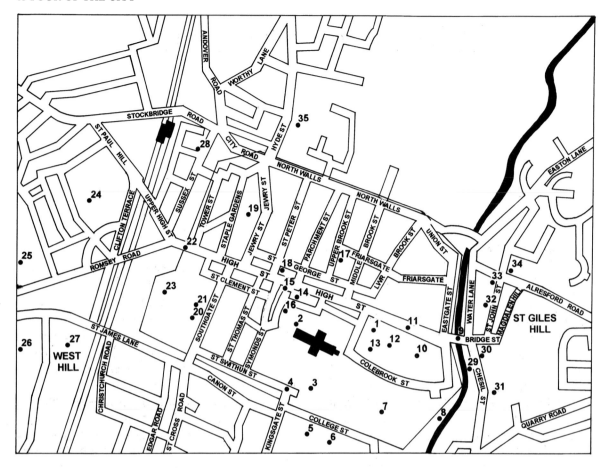

78 *Map showing the sites and monuments referred to in the tour (drawn by Philip Marter).*

bank, which marks the limit of an incomplete outer circuit of city defences. Otherwise the suburb contains a fine collection of nine-teenth-century institutional structures: hospital, prison *(25)*, training college *(26)*, and cemetery with gatehouse *(27)*, also some fine terraced and detached residences. At its junction with the northern suburb are found the railway station and the Hampshire Record Office (*28*; see **75**).

South

St Catharine's Hill and Twyford Down (now in part a stretch of the M3) are both significant prehistoric sites which lie to the south of the city. St Catharine's Hill (see **11**) is topped by a maze marked on the ground. Also to the south of the city lies the village of St Cross (see **34**), formerly Sparkford, with the medieval hospital and brothers' lodgings of the twelfth to fifteenth century (summer 09.30–12.30, 14.00–17.00; winter 10.30–12.30, 14.00–15.30). The walk through the watermeadows to St Cross inspired Keats to write his poem 'To Autumn'. Remains of the Itchen Navigation, especially St Catharine's lock, are of interest and can form part of a walk south of the city to St Catharine's Hill. There are fine nineteenth-century streets and churches, especially Christ Church and Christchurch Road, in the western area of the suburb.

East

Beyond the City Bridge is the eastern suburb. In Chesil Street (right) is The Soke, a seventeenth-century house (*29;* see **3**). Next to it is the medieval church of St Peter, Chesil, now a theatre. Almost opposite is the Old Chesil Rectory, an unusual medieval building *(30)*. Behind it are relics of the Great Western (Chesil) station yard and tunnels *(31)*. In St John Street is the eponymous church *(32)*, the best-preserved medieval parish church in the city, above it is The Blue Boar (*33*; see **44**), a fourteenth-century hall house. St John's Croft across the road is a splendid Georgian house *(34)*. Proceed up the hill to St Giles Hill, site of the medieval fair and with unrivalled panoramic views of the city. Beyond St Giles Hill is Winnall (now a housing and industrial estate) where signifi-cant prehistoric, Roman and Saxon cemeteries have been found.

North

To the north lies the suburb of Hyde. The largest Roman ceme-teries were here and remains of the abbey of Hyde *(35)* which removed there from the centre of town *c.* 1110. Fragments of abbey stonework are to be seen in adjacent buildings and in the church of St Bartholomew. An unmarked grave in the church-yard beside the east window may contain remains of King Alfred, scattered at the Reformation. The Hyde Historic Resources cen-tre is at 75 Hyde Street, and houses the Winchester City Museum Service and its extensive collections of photographs, local history room and the offices of the City Archaeologist.

Winchester chronology

10,000–3700 BC: Palaeolithic and Mesolithic: Winchester area not a focus of population

3700–2000 BC: Neolithic: marked increase in activity both within the area later walled-in and on the surrounding hills

2000–700 BC: Bronze Age: activity all round the city from *c.* 2000 BC

700–300 BC: Early Iron Age: agricultural settlements in the area; hill-fort at St Catharine's Hill

c. 600–300 BC: settlement at Erdberi (Oram's Arbour)

c. 300–100 BC: Middle Iron Age: settlements on downland of Itchen valley; Erdberi enclosed

c. 100 BC–AD 43: Late Iron Age: St Catharine's hill-fort abandoned (*c.* 100 BC); dense population and industrial activity at Erdberi followed by decline

AD 43: Roman invasion of Britain by Claudius: Romans settle area of Venta beside Itchen (*c.* 50)

After *c.* 70: Venta Belgarum accorded *civitas* status

c. 75: defences built on north, south (including South Gate) and west

100s: population 3–4000: town-house culture (to *c.* 350)

c. 150: first written reference to Venta Belgarum

c. 180–200: earthwork defences enclose *c.* 58ha (144 acres), including east perimeter

Before 200: Itchen diverted and bridged east of the city

300s: bastions added to defences

c. 330–50: possible Christian chi-rho motif in archaeological record alongside paganism

c. 350: textile *gynaecaeum* based at 'Venta'; town-house culture declining

Late 300s: great town houses demolished/adapted

c. 390–410: first Saxon cemeteries

c. 400–50: little archaeological evidence

After 500: pagan Saxon cemeteries outside city walls

Late 500s/early 600s: South Gate blocked

c. 600 to after 700: Saxon cemeteries continue

635: arrival of Christian missionary Birinus in Wessex

642–73: King Cenwalh reigns: return of Christianity

648: traditional date for foundation of Old Minster

660: Bishop Wine, the first known bishop of Winchester, appointed

c. 650–700: Christian female burial at Lower Brook Street

c. 700: foundation of Saxon Southampton

757: first reference to Hampshire, earliest shire

860: Vikings attack Winchester

861x3: death of Bishop Swithun

871–99: reign of King Alfred: Winchester mint evidence late in

reign; buried at Winchester

896: Alfred's only recorded visit to Winchester

899–924: reign of Edward the Elder; buried at Winchester

901: foundation of New Minster

963: Bishop Aethelwold (died 984) elected to Winchester by King Edgar (959–75)

Before 980: establishment of Wolvesey bishop's residence

980: rededication of Old Minster, converted to monasticism, by Aethelwold

1016–35: reign of Cnut: buried at Old Minster

1042: Harthacnut buried at Winchester

c. 1057: population of city 5500–8000

1066: battle of Hastings and Norman Conquest: Winchester opens its gates to the Conqueror

1069: rebellion against William I: Stigand removed as Bishop of Winchester and Archbishop of Canterbury (1070) and imprisoned at new Winchester Castle (1072)

1079–80: Winchester Cathedral begun by Bishop Walkelin (1070–98)

1093: dedication of the cathedral, otherwise St Swithun's priory church; Swithun's remains transferred from Old Minster which was demolished

1100–29: William Giffard bishop: building at cathedral and Wolvesey

1107: cathedral tower collapses

c. 1110: survey of Winchester: 1300 houses, second only to London; New Minster moves to northern suburb at Hyde

1129–71: Henry of Blois bishop: building at Wolvesey; St Cross (*c.* 1135); Winchester Bible (*c.* 1160)

1135–54: reign of Stephen: civil war and anarchy: city besieged and severely damaged (1141)

1148: survey of Winchester: 1100 houses; 57 parish churches

1154–89: reign of Henry II: royal 'Hawkeye' built north-west of city; castle works (1170s)

1189–99: reign of Richard I: coronations at Winchester in 1189 and 1194; charter

1199–1216: reign of John; reign ends in civil war and with siege of castle; charter

c. 1200: city seal shows crenellated gates; first reference to a mayor

1205–38: Peter des Roches bishop

1207: Henry III (reigned 1216–72) born at Winchester

1222–36: castle Great Hall built, Peter des Roches a prime mover

1227: Henry III of age: charter promises perpetual mint at Winchester

1231: Bishop des Roches returns to England, establishes The Soke – separate jurisdiction

1248–50: final removal of mint

1250–60: Aymer of Lusignan (de Valence) bishop: created rich Purbeck screen to enclose Swithun's shrine

1258: barons beseige bishop in Wolvesey

1261: Winchester parliament in Great Hall

1264: citizens attack priory burning King's and Prior's Gates; Henry III acts to protect Jews in the city

1265: capture of city by Simon de Montfort the younger

1285: Statute of Winchester

1290: expulsion of Jews by Edward I (1272–1307)

c. 1290: date for wood of Round Table and of earliest dated timber-framed house in the city

c. 1300: population in range 8000–11,625

1302: royal visit and fire at castle

1326–53: Winchester a wool staple town

1338–9: wall works inspired by recent French raids

1345–66: William Edington bishop; demolishes Norman westworks of cathedral (*c.* 1350)

1348–50: Black Death kills 48 per cent of clergy in Winchester diocese; serious effects in the city

1366–1404: William of Wykeham bishop

1369: royal order for repair of walls

1377–99: Richard II king: visits Winchester 1393

1377–81: poll tax levied

1377: French land on south coast; Durn Gate walled up on ward alderman's orders

1381: Great (or Peasants') Revolt: violence in Winchester

1382: Wykeham receives royal licence to obtain lands for Winchester College

1387–1401: Chamber Court (1387–94) and Outer Court (1397–1401) at Winchester College built

1393: parliament summoned to Winchester

1399–1413: Henry IV king; visits Winchester in 1402 to marry Joan of Navarre

1417: tarrage roll evidence gives population of 7–8000

1440/52: petition twice sent to king complaining of 11 almost depopulated streets, 997 empty houses, 17 churches without incumbents etc.; withdrawal of cloth industry

1447–86: William Waynflete bishop

c. 1475–90: Waynflete's great screen in cathedral

1476: relics of Swithun paraded through the city *en route* to new shrine

1485: Henry VII first Tudor monarch: christening of Prince Arthur at Winchester (1486)

1493–1501: Thomas Langton bishop; died of plague; chantry chapel completed by Richard Fox (bishop 1501–28) has perhaps earliest Renaissance work in England

1522: Emperor Charles V visits Winchester with Henry VIII: probable date of painting of Round Table

1524: population 2000–4300

1531–51, 1553–5: Stephen Gardiner bishop

1530s: early attempt at Itchen navigation failed

1538–40: Dissolution of monasteries: destruction of Waynflete's screen, Swithun's shrine and monastic buildings at cathedral priory, Hyde and St Mary's Abbey, friaries etc.

1551: citizens acquire East Gate and income from its tolls from successors of dissolved St Mary's Abbey

1554: Queen Mary married to Philip of Spain in the cathedral

1566: tailors and hosiers seek protection against rural craftsmen

1579: county workhouse established at the castle with encouragement from Sir Francis Walsingham (made High Steward of city 1582)

1583: first outbreak of plague for almost 20 years

1588: Charter of Incorporation

1591 (and 1604): earliest references to horse racing at Winchester

1594, 1595: corporation bought wheat and rye for poor to eat; wool and flax for them to work for wages

1597: burials in St Maurice and in northern suburb reach epidemic proportions

1603: religious census found twice as many recusants as Nonconformists in Winchester: 1851 communicants

1603–6: plague in the city and suburbs

1615: Symonds's almshouse opens

1620s: Winchester fails to get Itchen navigation accepted

1625: worst plague since the Black Death

1632–47: Walter Curle bishop: oversaw creation of cathedral tower vault decorated c. 1635 with statues of James I and Charles I; Inigo Jones screen and Laudian altar canopy

1642–6: Civil War: city attacked and pillaged by both sides; royalists in castle surrender to Waller; city plundered by parliamentary soldiers who also sack shops and the cathedral (1642); Sir William Ogle holds castle for royalists (1644–5); parliamentarians under Waller defeat Hopton at Cheriton. Refugees flee to Winchester Castle; Cromwell arrives and takes suburbs without resistance; bombards castle; Ogle surrenders (1645); population falls to under 5000

1649: Charles I executed; royalist city government replaced

1651: castle demolished

1660: Restoration greeted with joy in the city; Catholic burials in St James cemetery begin

1660–2: Brian Duppa bishop: begins rebuilding at Wolvesey

1662–84: Bishop Morley repairs Wolvesey and donates his library to the cathedral; new houses built for clergy in The Close to replace those demolished during interregnum

1662: reforming commissioners eject the 1649 city government

1664: Itchen navigation included in a bill, but limited by Southampton's intervention to coal and 'the Norway trade'

1665: hearth tax: population estimate 5900

1665: Sir Robert Mason's Eastgate House built

1666: plague serious: pit-cairns still visible south of St Catharine's Hill

1668: hearth tax farmers cite Winchester as a city where receipts had fallen due to the plague

1674: nine canons lived in houses with ten or more hearths; Morley College for widows built

1676: Compton 'census': 3700 population estimated

1680s: Charles II's patronage makes city a centre for upper-class society

1682: Charles II and court attend races at Winchester: palace plans hatched

1685: Charles II dies: palace building halts: 138ha (342 acres) in royal hands

1686: stabling and bed survey: Winchester far better off than any other Hampshire town with stabling for 1000+ horses

1704: 90 shops assessed within the walls for land tax; 20 substantial houses in the city

1714: new guildhall sponsored by Queen Anne

1720: mayor refuses to co-operate with bishop to expel numerous Catholic families because of their 'great advantage' to the city

1725: visitation suggests rising population especially in suburbs: 4000

1750: first measured map of Winchester, by Godson

1771: Winchester Pavement Commission established to oversee paving and lighting of streets

1788: visitation returns: population of 3500–4000

1801: census gives figure of 5826

1838: Corn Exchange, Jewry Street opens

1839: Southampton Railway opens

1840: Diocesan Training College founded; London railway opens

1841: census gives population of 10,732

1845: British Archaeological Association and Institute meet in Winchester

1845–52: Carter reworks Great Hall and remodels Grand Jury Chamber, Castle Yard

1851: census gives population of 13,335; Bishop's Cheyney Court ceased to function

1872: large-scale Ordnance Survey map of the city

1873: new guildhall completed in The Broadway

1875: sewage-pumping station established at Garnier Road

1885: Didcot, Newbury and Southampton Junction Railway opens in Winchester

1888: creation of Hampshire County Council

1891: census gives population of 17,179

1894: fire destroys Charles II's palace

1901: population census: 21,702

1903: opening of Winchester Museum, The Square

1914–18: World War I: 460 citizens of Winchester gave their lives in a tradition of 'service and sacrifice handed down from the days of King Alfred'

1920s: new housing at Stanmore wins national acclaim

1928: Diocesan Training College becomes King Alfred's College

1930s: Depression, little building in the city

1939–45: World War II: Dunkirk evacuees housed at Barracks; Winchester bypass a valuable transport link, especially for D-Day preparations (1944); destruction and post-war depression provide an opportunity for archaeology

1951: population census: 25,721

1959: Queen Elizabeth Court County Council buildings opened

1961–71: Winchester Excavations Committee organizes archaeology in the city

1971: population census: 31,107

Late 1980s: Winchester dubbed 'the wealthiest city in Britain'

1991: population census: 29,758

1990s: 'rescue' and 'research' archaeology in the city give way to planning-led work; Twyford Down 'revolt' characterizes local concerns and growing awareness of historic environment

Further reading

Publications relating to Winchester, including books, museum newsletters and journal articles from a broad range of publications are listed in *Winchester: a bibliography* by Susan C. Browne (Winchester Project, King Alfred's College, 1993). This is available through the Hampshire County Library Service and from the Hampshire Record Office. It is in two parts, organized by subject and by author. The following works are particularly recommended:

M. Biddle (ed.) *Winchester in the Early Middle Ages: an edition and discussion of the Winton Domesday,* Winchester Studies 1 (Oxford, 1976)

M. Biddle, 'The Study of Winchester: archaeology and history in a British town, 1961–1983', *Proceedings of the British Academy* 69 (1983), pp. 93–135

M. Biddle, *Wolvesey: the old bishop's palace, Winchester* (London, 1986)

M. Biddle (ed.) *Object and Economy in Medieval Winchester,* Winchester Studies 7.ii (Oxford, 1990)

M. Biddle and B. Clayre, *Winchester Castle and Great Hall* (Hampshire County Council, 1983)

B. Carpenter Turner, *Winchester* (Chichester, reprinted 1990)

G. Clarke, *Pre-Roman and Roman Winchester, Part II: The Roman Cemetery at Lankhills,* Winchester Studies 3.ii (Oxford, 1979)

J. Collis, *Winchester Excavations 1949–60,* volume ii (Winchester, 1978)

J. Crook, *Winchester Cathedral: Nine Hundred Years* (Chichester, 1993)

B. Cunliffe, *Winchester Excavations 1949–1960,* volume i (Winchester, 1964)

T. B. James, *Winchester: a pictorial history* (Chichester, 1993)

D. J. Keene, *Survey of Medieval Winchester,* Winchester Studies 2 (Oxford, 1985)

E. Lewis, E. Roberts and K. Roberts, *Medieval Hall Houses of the Winchester Area* (Winchester, 1988)

N. Pevsner and D. Lloyd, *Hampshire,* Buildings of England series (London, 1967)

K. E. Qualmann, 'Roman Winchester' in S. Greep (ed.) *Roman Towns: the Wheeler inheritance,* CBA Research Report 93 (1993)

A. Rosen, 'Winchester in Transition 1580–1700' in P. Clark (ed.) *Country Towns in Pre-Industrial England* (Leicester, 1981)

G. Scobie and K. Qualmann, *Nunnaminster: a Saxon and medieval community of nuns* (Winchester, 1993)

G. D. Scobie, J. M. Zant and R. Whinney, *The Brooks, Winchester: a preliminary report on the excavations 1987–88,* Winchester Museums Service – Archaeology Report 1 (Winchester, 1991)

Index

The Author

Dr Tom Beaumont James is a graduate of St Andrews University and is currently Reader in History and Archaeology at King Alfred's College of Higher Education in Winchester. He has been elected to fellowships of the Society of Antiquaries of Scotland (1976), the Society of Antiquaries of London (1980) and to the Royal Historical Society (1990). Apart from medieval studies and nineteenth-century art his pastimes include travel and cricket. He is married to a publisher and they have three sons.

This volume is part of a major series, jointly conceived for English Heritage and Batsford, under the general editorship of Dr Stephen Johnson at English Heritage.

Titles in the series:

Sites
Avebury Caroline Malone
Danebury Barry Cunliffe
Dover Castle Jonathan Coad
Flag Fen: Prehistoric Fenland Centre Francis Pryor
Fountains Abbey Glyn Coppack
Glastonbury Philip Rahtz
Hadrian's Wall Stephen Johnson
Housesteads James Crow
Ironbridge Gorge Catherine Clark
Lindisfarne Deirdre O'Sullivan and Robert Young
Maiden Castle Niall M. Sharples
Roman Bath Barry Cunliffe
Roman London Gustav Milne
Roman York Patrick Ottaway
Stonehenge Julian Richards
Tintagel Charles Thomas
The Tower of London Geoffrey Parnell
Viking Age York Richard Hall
Wharram Percy: Deserted Medieval Village Maurice Beresford and John Hurst
Forthcoming
St Augustine's Abbey Richard Gem et al.

Periods
Anglo-Saxon England Martin Welch
Bronze Age Britain Michael Parker Pearson
Iron Age Britain Barry Cunliffe
Roman Britain Martin Millett
Viking Age England Julian D. Richards
Forthcoming
Industrial England Michael Stratton and Barrie Trinder
Norman England Trevor Rowley
Stone Age Britain Nick Barton

Subjects
Abbeys and Priories Glyn Coppack
Canals Nigel Crowe
Castles Tom McNeill
Channel Defences Andrew Saunders
Church Archaeology Warwick Rodwell
Life in Roman Britain Joan Alcock
Prehistoric Settlements Robert Bewley
Roman Towns in Britain Guy de la Bédoyère
Roman Villas and the Countryside Guy de la Bédoyère
Shrines and Sacrifice Ann Woodward
Victorian Churches James Stevens Curl
Forthcoming
Roman Forts in Britain Paul Bidwell
Seaside Architecture Simon Adamson
Ships and Shipwrecks Peter Marsden

Towns
Canterbury Marjorie Lyle
Chester Peter Carrington
Durham Martin Roberts
Norwich Brian Ayers
Winchester Tom Beaumont James
York Richard Hall

Landscapes
Forthcoming
The Cotswolds Timothy Darvill and Alan McWhirr
Dartmoor Sandy Gerrard
The Peak District John Barnatt and Ken Smith
The Yorkshire Dales Robert White

'One of the great classic series of British archaeology.' *Current Archaeology*

KING ALFRED'S COLLEGE
LIBRARY